God Rest Ye Merry

God Rest Ye
MERRY

Why Christmas is the Foundation for Everything

DOUGLAS WILSON

canonpress
Moscow, Idaho

Douglas Wilson, *God Rest Ye Merry:*
Why Christmas is the Foundation for Everything
Copyright © 2012 by Douglas Wilson.

Published by Canon Press
P.O. Box 8729, Moscow, ID 83843
800.488.2034 | www.canonpress.com

Cover design by Rachel Rosales.
Interior design by Laura Storm Design.
Printed in the United States of America.

Unless otherwise indicated, Scripture quotations are from the King James Version of the Bible.

Library of Congress Cataloging-in-Publication Data

Wilson, Douglas, 1953-
  God rest ye merry : Why Christmas is the foundation for everything /
Douglas Wilson.
    p. cm.
  ISBN 978-1-59128-127-6
  1. Christmas. 2. Advent--Meditations. I. Title.
  BV45.W545 2012
  232.92--dc23
                                          2012039204

13 14 15 16 17 18 19 20   10 9 8 7 6 5 4 3 2

This book is for Gordon and Meredith,
and family—all you guys!
Merry Christmas!

CONTENTS

PREFACE

This small book is broken up into five lessons, or sections. The first deals with the foundational doctrines that are connected to the Christmas story. If Jesus Christ is the cornerstone—and He is—the Christmas story tells how the first preparations were made to lay that stone. The second section addresses a fact too commonly overlooked, which is the inherently political nature of the Christmas story, a fact that Herod understood better than we frequently do. The third lesson brings up some historical considerations—is it possible to really celebrate Christmas in a robust fashion, and yet honor our Puritan heritage? Didn't the Puritans have a Scrooge-like approach to Christmas? Well, yes and no. The fourth section concerns the much lamented "materialism" of Christmas, and addresses the problem by suggesting that the chin-pulling laments over "consumerism" are actually more of a threat to the true meaning of Christmas than all the plasma televisions are. And last, the final section is a series of daily meditations for the Advent season, accompanied with a prayer—suitable for use as family readings during the Advent season.

TO GAIN HIS EVERLASTING HALL

If the history of the world is a story, then theology is a type of literary criticism. We do not just read the story and go with the flow of it, we are also to reflect on it as we read. What is the meaning of the story? We do not just want to know that the infinite God was born as a baby at Bethlehem, we should also want to know what that staggering reality might mean. Of course we must include the great events—creation, fall, the flood, the exile to Babylon. And when we include them, we must rank them, and if we do that, the birth of the Christ in Bethlehem is one of the greatest plot points ever. In this first section, we will give ourselves to reflections on what an odd thing the Incarnation was. How so?

TO GAIN HIS EVERLASTING HALL

Bethlehem was the opening gambit in the last campaign of a long war. Many centuries after our father Adam had first plunged our race into the insanity of sin, God finally made His opening move. Jesus Christ, born of a woman, born under law, was born to fulfill every one of the numerous promises that God had made during our long night.

At the beginning of our world, scarcely had our race fallen into sin and darkness but our Father God swore that the seed of the woman would have vengeance upon the serpent, promising us a glorious deliverance. And so, for long ages, the faithful looked ahead to that undefined day—figuring, studying, mentally groping, but fundamentally trusting. What form would the dragon slayer take? What form would the serpent worm have in the day when his head was finally crushed?

The servants of God, earthly and celestial both, were well aware of the great obstacles, but knew at the same time that the wisdom of God was far greater than any obstacle. But although they knew this, the campaign plans were still highly classified. The apostle Peter describes it this way:

> Of which salvation the prophets have enquired and searched diligently, who prophesied of the grace that should come unto you: Searching what, or what manner of time the Spirit of Christ which was in them did signify, when it testified beforehand the sufferings of Christ, and the glory that should follow. Unto whom

it was revealed, that not unto themselves, but unto us they did minister the things, which are now reported unto you by them that have preached the gospel unto you with the Holy Ghost sent down from heaven; which things the angels desire to look into. (1 Pet. 1:10–12)

It has always been like this. Our good God, our overflowing God, our God of *yes* and *amen*, has always been able to promise far more than we are able to believe. I am not here speaking of unbelief, or of hard hearts, which is another problem. I am speaking here of a true and sincere faith, a God-given faith, but one which is still finite, and which God loves to bury under an avalanche of promises. We serve and worship the God who overwhelms, who *delights* to overwhelm. At His right hand are pleasures forevermore—a cascading waterfall of infinite pleasures, with no top, no bottom, no back, no front, and no sides. Nothing but infinite pleasure in motion, and every one of those pleasures is attached to His promises.

What does the apostle Paul tell us about the salvation that this God would introduce into our history, into our story?

Howbeit we speak wisdom among them that are perfect: yet not the wisdom of this world, nor of the princes of this world, that come to nought: But we speak the wisdom of God in a mystery, even the hidden wisdom, which God ordained before the world unto our glory: Which none of the princes of this world knew: for had they known it, they would not have crucified the Lord of glory. But as it is written, Eye hath not seen, nor ear heard, neither have entered into the heart of man, the things which God hath prepared for them that love him. But God hath revealed them unto us by his Spirit: for the Spirit searcheth all things, yea, the deep things of God. For what man knoweth the things of a man, save the spirit of man which is in him? Even so the things of God knoweth no man, but the Spirit of God. (1 Cor. 2:6–11)

Because these promises stagger us, we have developed a work-around, something to keep us from feeling the crushing weight of God's promised goodness to our world. That workaround consists of pushing the fulfillment of His promises out past the day of resurrection, safely storing them all in a time when we are allowed not to think about it. But this passage from Paul is not talking about the eternal state. It has nothing to do with the eternal state. He lived in the third chapter, we live in the tenth chapter, and he was talking about the fifteenth chapter. He was not talking about the next book, the one we shall all read in the resurrection. These are promises concerning our future history.

And so it is always thus—our poets and seers see more than we do. They write poems and hymns, they write carols that are un-inspired, but are prophetic utterances nonetheless. Just as Isaiah spoke far beyond what he could grasp, so also did Wesley. Just as the Jews memorized and chanted the words of Isaiah, words that were beyond their grasp, so also we have memorized carols that speak of the depth of glory that is coming, and we are always singing out of our depth. We are not singing about what will happen after the resurrection. We sing about the years to come, here, in our midst. We are singing about promises and blessings that *will* overtake our children's children.

I do not say this by way of chiding or blame. As we have noted, the apostle Paul said that it was *designed* this way—eye has not seen, and ear has not heard, what God has prepared for those who love Him. Do you love Him? Then *brace* yourself, and sing to a world that needs to brace itself.

We were in desperate straits. Christ came to "ransom captive Israel" and to "disperse the gloomy clouds of night." In our inso-lence, we were "doomed by law to endless woe" and were neces-sarily and justly consigned to "the dreadful gulf below." But this darkness we had created was invaded by the heavenly host, "Rank on rank the host of heaven spreads its vanguard on the way," and the night above the shepherds lit up as though a lightning bolt had refused to go out, had refused to stop shining. The road *was* weary, but now we may urge others to "rest beside the weary road, and hear the angels sing." We needed this salvation just as He gave it. "O Savior, King of glory, who dost our weakness know." The God who knows our frame timed it perfectly.

And so the ache was healed. "In Bethlehem, in Israel, this blessed babe was born." *This* was "Israel's strength and consolation," *He* was the "dear desire of every nation." "Now He shines, the long expected," and "glories stream from heaven afar."

All creation is summoned to rejoice. He is the "high born King of ages"—"Word of the Father, now in flesh appearing." Nothing whatever is excluded; we invite "all that grows beneath the shining of the moon and burning sun" to join in our praise. This gospel is proclaimed, and the antiphon is sung by the "mountains in reply." All of it bursts forth—both "heav'n and nature sing." This is right and fitting because "he comes to make His blessings flow, far as the curse is found." All cursed things may sing *this* blessing.

The *nations* are gathered before Him. On behalf of those nations, He is "ris'n with healing in His wings," and so we summon all the nations to join us. "Joyful all ye nations rise, join the triumph of the skies." Africa, come! We urge the Far East not to tarry. South America, behold your Lord. And we beseech our own nations to repent our apostasies and turn back to Him again. This is not optional; the poets have commanded it. "He makes the nations prove the glories of His righteousness." The saints of God are therefore insistent. "Powers, dominions, bow before Him," as we declare "honor, glory, and dominion, and eternal victory." We lean into the future expectantly, looking forward to the time "when with the ever circling years, comes round the age of gold."

"With the dawn of redeeming grace," what is the only possible response? We gather to "hymn and chant with high thanksgiving," and however high the thanksgiving is, the object of our praise is higher still. "Come, peasant, king, to own Him." We praise Him, and He calls us—"calls you one and calls you all, to gain His everlasting hall." And in the skies above that everlasting hall, the ascending hymns fill up "the endless day."

Indeed, "Nor eye hath seen, nor ear / Hath yet attained to hear / What there is ours."

"O come let us adore Him, Christ the Lord."

Amen, and amen. In the name of the Father, Son, and Holy Spirit, *amen again.*

CHRISTMAS IRONY

At Christmastime, we are privileged to reflect on how God in His wisdom has taken human sophistication and urbanity, and folded it back over itself, turning everything around. The first Christmas was the time in history when God began announcing His mastery of irony—and it is also the time when the worldly wise began their fruitless attempts to studiously ignore what He was doing. And in this attempt, they shut themselves off from that laughter that William Tyndale described as coming from the "low bottom of the heart."

Christian literary scholar Anthony Esolen has identified three principal uses of irony—uses that God Himself has displayed richly in the Incarnation, and which faithful Christians have been imitating ever since. They are the irony of time, the irony of power, and the irony of love. God is a masterful writer, and so the Christian faith is therefore the central source of deep, understated, rich and lyrical irony. We love what words can do because we love what the Word has done.

Our postmodern age likes to pretend *it* has mastered irony simply because our late night comedians have mastered the cheap shots of cynicism, the ability to point—as the fellow said—to the price of everything and the value of nothing. But this is not the kind of thing we mean at all. Our use of irony, if it is to be Christian, must be an harmonious echo of what God has done in Christ.

First, let's consider the irony of time. In John Buchan's novel *Mr. Standfast*, the central character says that he would trust to Providence because, as a friend of his had put it, "Providence was all right if you gave him a chance." Twists and turns in the plot are to be expected because there *is* a plot, one devised by a master. For the ancient pagans, history was not history at all, but simply a long, recurring, endless cycle, or a meaningless clash of meaningless fated events. They assumed that atomistic fragmentation represented the whole fairly accurately—what you saw was what you got. But Christians, looking at the same phenomena, concluded something quite different. All these strange elements, seemingly headed in every which direction, meant, of necessity that the last chapter of our world's story was going to be *the* ultimate denouement. If all things work together for good for them that love God and are called according to His purpose, then this means that billions of plot points are going to come together in the most satisfying cathartic release possible at the end of all time. The great day of resurrection, the eschatological climax, will be what Tolkien called eucatastrophe, and will be literary catharsis writ large, although *large* is far too small a word for it.

Bethlehem is the moment in the story when significant numbers of readers start to have that *aha* moment. The consummate writer, God foreshadows what He is going to do; in fact, He was doing that from the earliest prophets on. But at Bethlehem, the central character arrives in the story, and those following the story recognize Him. Those who recognize Him this way are called believers, and as the story unfolds, there will be more and more of us. By the last chapter, every knee will bow and every tongue will confess Him. But in this grand denouement at the end, not only will everyone see who He is, but we will also all see who He has been all along, and we shall see that history, far from being a tale told by an idiot, full of sound and fury, signifying nothing, is actually the ultimate ironic tale. Christ as the Word is the irony of time, He is the irony of story. In worshiping Christ, in worshiping the *Word*, Christians are worshiping God's irony.

Second, we should also reflect on the irony of power. *How* did God choose to enter the story He was writing? God overcame the world and its evil forces by setting aside His omnipotence, and becoming a helpless baby. The Incarnate One now had pitiful limbs, had tiny arms and legs, but even *they* were bound up tight in the swaddling clothes that Mary had remembered to bring with her. God was taking on what Martin Luther once called "left-handed power," the authority that arises naturally from a certain kind of willed helplessness. We are not talking about the helplessness that is simply impotence fueled by cowardice. Rather, we are recognizing how to overcome evil with good, how a strong man turns the other cheek, how the one who could have called for legions of angels to rescue Him from the cross declined to do so. The one who took the position of servant was given authority over all. The one who humbled Himself to the point of death was given a name above every name.

The one who spoke the galaxies into existence at the beginning of all things took on human flesh and consented to have his diapers changed. But He did not do this in order to demonstrate how low He could stoop, as though that stooping were arbitrary or aimless. Rather, He ordained that stooping this low would be the means by which He overcame the world. And He ordained that stooping in this way would be the means by which His disciples followed Him into the kingdom.

So Bethlehem is the place where every thoughtful person must wonder: *what* is He doing? And when we think we know, it is only because we have gotten used to the idea in that setting. But whenever we see someone imitating God's ways in this—at our place of employment perhaps—we are as startled as ever.

And last, the irony of love. St. John tells us that God so loved the world that He gave us His only begotten Son. That giving began at Bethlehem, was continued in His perfect sinless life as the new Israel, and culminated at the cross where He died for our sins. He entered into His joy (and our justification) at His resurrection, and He now sits at the right hand of God the Father, where there is a torrent of pleasure forever. He *is* that cascading torrent of pleasure. He *is* that endless waterfall of joy, which is hard for us to visualize because there is no top, and no bottom, and no sides. But there is an endless motion of delight just the same, and because we are in Christ, we are right in the middle of it.

So love sacrifices, but love never sacrifices at a dead end. There have been many sacrifices that *look* like a dead end—remember the ironies of time—but they are not at all what they appear to be. What could have been more of a dead end than to be flogged, crucified, speared, and laid in a grave for three days and nights? And yet, even there, God was demonstrating His love for us. He was not giving us one more tragedy in a long line of them so that we might be justified in our despair. Rather, He was conquering sin and death, lust and the devil—and *not* giving us a lesson in pointless heroism.

And so this is the meaning of Christmas, a meaning which lines up perfectly with the meaning of the rest of the story. God is an ironist. He folds the story up in unexpected ways, tying things together that we could never have imagined. He is the ironist of time, of history, of story. He, in possession of ultimate right-handed power, determined to set it all aside, and overcame evil by taking on an invincible vulnerability, inviting us to learn how to do the same. He is not just strong, but also wise in the authority of humility. And He is love, which means He overflows in sacrificial ways. But His sacrifices are not throwaways, but always come back to Him thirty, sixty, and a hundredfold. Love is fruitful, and in imitation of Him we begin to learn that the more we give, the more we have.

This Christmas, remember you are learning how to open God's gifts to us. And because He really knows how to shop for us, when we get the wrapping paper off, we are *always* surprised.

MYSTERY OF INCARNATION

Godly summaries of biblical teaching are inescapable, whatever we may call them. They may be creeds, catechisms, systematic theologies or sermons, but when it is done properly, the result is consistently honoring to God. But of course, we need to take care to learn what "done properly" means from the pages of Scripture itself. Thus, passages in the Bible which summarize the message of the Bible are of great value to us:

> And without controversy great is the mystery of godliness: God was manifest in the flesh, justified in the Spirit, seen of angels, preached unto the Gentiles, believed on in the world, received up into glory. (1 Tim. 3:16)

In discussing these things there is no controversy about one aspect: the mystery of godliness is *great*. Note that what follows is described in two ways. First, it is a great mystery. Secondly, it is a great mystery concerning piety or godliness. But what follows are assertions that we would not typically relate to piety. This is because we have confused moralism with morality, pietism with piety, smarminess with godliness, and, at the end of the day, death with life.

First, God was manifest in the flesh. Secondly, this Jesus was justified in the Spirit through His resurrection. Third, angels saw

Him. Fourth, He was preached to the Gentiles. Fifth, men in this dark world actually believed what was preached. Sixth, our Lord Jesus was received up into heavenly glory.

What is the great mystery of godliness? What is the foundation of our salvation? *God* was manifest in the *flesh*.

We sometimes do not appreciate the magnitude of the problem here. How could the eternal Word of the eternal Father take on limits? How can infinitude and finitude marry? The doctrine of the Incarnation proclaims frankly and without embarrassment the most stupendous miracle that can be imagined. Veiled in flesh the Godhead see, hail the Incarnate Deity.

But we are dealing with mysteries and miracles, not contradictions. We are not maintaining that Jesus was God and was simultaneously not God in the same respect that He was God. We are saying that our Savior, Jesus of Nazareth, was and is one person, but a person with two natures—divine and human. These two natures do not run together in a confused way, but neither are they separated in such a way as to make Jesus the ultimate schizophrenic, two persons cobbled together.

That which is predicated of the one nature can also be predicated of the person: "Jesus is God." That which is predicated of the other nature can be predicated of the person: "Jesus was from the tribe of Judah." That which is predicated of the one nature should *not* be predicated of the other nature: "Humanity is Deity." This important barrier was established for us in the decision of the council of Chalcedon.

This text also shows us the meaning of ultimate justification. We are told here that "God manifest in the flesh" was "justified in the Spirit." We are told in Scripture that this justification was accomplished by the Holy Spirit in the resurrection of Christ from the dead. "And declared *to be* the Son of God with power, according to the spirit of holiness, by the resurrection from the dead" (Rom. 1:4). This justification was *of* Christ, vindicating and declaring who He was and is. But it was also *for* us, because all that Christ has and is is imputed to us—we are members of His body, of His flesh and of His bones. "Now it was not written for his sake alone, that it was imputed to him; but for us also, to whom it shall be imputed, if we believe on him that raised up Jesus our Lord from the dead; who was delivered for our offences, and was raised again for our justification" (Rom. 4:23–25). The power of the gospel is resident here, in this. The power at work within us is the same power that God used in raising Jesus from the dead (Eph. 1:19–20).

So, all things are ours. The resurrection of Jesus Christ, which was *His* justification, was also for *our* justification. In the declaration that Jesus was the Son of God we are declared to be sons of God. This, incidentally, shows the glory of imputation. This is an insistence that we have not yet begun to dream about what has been imputed to us. "Therefore let no man glory in men. For all things are yours; whether Paul, or Apollos, or Cephas, or the world, or life, or death, or things present, or things to come; all are yours; and ye are Christ's; and Christ *is* God's" (1 Cor. 3:21–23).

Christ is seen, preached, and believed. When the angels saw the resurrected Christ, they did not see an abstract doctrine. They saw *Him*. When we preach this, we do not preach a mere doctrine. We preach *Him*. When sinners believe, they do not just believe a doctrine. They believe *Him*. What is the difference?

Looked at from the side, all Christian preaching and teaching is made up of nouns, verbs, propositions, questions, and so on. In just the same way, the bread and wine of the Lord's Supper remain simply bread and wine. If a chemist were to scurry around the table when we are meeting with Christ there, he would find nothing but the regular stuff. And if a grammarian or logician were to break apart and analyze the "stuff" of preaching, he would find assertions and doctrines, nouns and verbs. He would see the form, but not the power. But saving faith, godly trust, does not stare *at*. Faith looks *through*. And so, children of God, behold your God.

The last statement of our scriptural summary is that Jesus Christ was received up into glory. This glory of His is not limited to heaven. He pours it out, He bestows it, He imputes it to us. Everything that can be done with this glory *is* done, and it is done on our behalf. "But we all, with open face beholding as in a glass the glory of the Lord, are changed into the same image from glory to glory, *even* as by the Spirit of the Lord" (2 Cor. 3:18). How do we see the glory of the Lord with open face? Where do we meet with Him? Where do we see Him? When do we converse with Him? The gift of faith is what you are doing in the moment you hear the Word. You are preparing for the sacrament. You are celebrating the fact that God was first manifested in the flesh inside the flesh of another, His mother Mary.

In this season of Advent, do you see your God?

THE SONG OF MARY

The Bible teaches us a great deal about our Lord's mother, and about her great and astonishing faith. But unfortunately, Roman Catholic errors, idolatries, and excesses have created or contributed to a great overreaction from Protestants, and hence a great loss for us. Often we do not even want to talk about Mary at all, still less with the great honor she deserves, for fear of being thought of as drifting toward the folly of assuming she is somehow *co-redemptrix* or *co-mediatrix* with her Son. One of Rome's great sins is that of chasing evangelical Christians away from Mary. But the Scripture remains clear in its testimony, at least. "And in the sixth month the angel Gabriel was sent from God unto a city of Galilee, named Nazareth " (Lk. 1:26–56).

Mary really was blessed among all women. It would be difficult for Luke to have communicated his theme any more clearly. When Gabriel appears, he says she is blessed among women (v. 8). She has found favor with God (v. 30). Elizabeth, inspired by the Holy Spirit, pronounces her blessed among women again (v. 42). Elizabeth blesses her again in verse 45. Mary herself recognizes that all future generations will call her blessed (v. 48). If some have distorted this blessing by claiming too much for her, it is hardly fitting for us to distort the blessing through doing something else. Above all, what the Word plainly teaches is to be our guide in such things.

What was the character of Mary? Scripture does not tell us how old Mary was, but if she was typical of young marriageable women of her time, she could have been around fourteen years old. And in no way does the portrait painted by Luke represent her to us as a silly little thing. Quite the reverse.

We learn she was a woman in need of a Savior: Mary knows of her need for forgiveness. She refers here to God as her *Savior* (v. 47). The thought that she was personally sinless and immaculately conceived had never entered her head. Nor should it enter ours. She was a woman of faith: Mary considers what Gabriel says and immediately submits herself to it (v. 38). And Elizabeth blesses Mary as one who *believed* (v. 45). In her song, she showed that she was dependent upon the promises of Scripture. The angelic messenger was no substitute for the Word. God had helped Israel, and He had done so in accordance with the promises to the fathers (vv. 54–55). And at the center of her faith was the promise made to Abraham (v. 55). Mary was quite evidently a woman of the Word: this Magnificat is made up almost entirely of language from the Old Testament, and shows a deep and thorough knowledge of Scripture. In particular, we are reminded of Hannah's song (1 Sam. 2:1–10). Not only does Mary's language echo the language of many passages from the Old Testament, but she also refers to God's saving acts recounted there (vv. 50–52). She was a woman of deep humility: Mary knew that she was selected to be the mother of the Messiah from a "low estate" (v. 48). She does not interpret the blessing that was given to her in a prideful or arrogant way. And crowning all of it, she was a woman of gratitude: her soul immediately turned to "magnify the Lord" (v. 46). She rejoiced in her God and Savior (v. 47). God had done great things for her, which she is careful to recount (v. 49).

Not only was Mary blessed, but so was her Son (v. 42). Mary overcame in the way women are called to conquer—by giving birth to conquerors, or by giving birth to daughters who will give birth to conquerors. And this explains how the Magnificat can have been composed by a woman and still be so gloriously *militant*. Godly child-bearing *is* militant. The seed of the *woman* has crushed the dragon's head.

And so, at Christmas, how are we called to imitate Mary, as we treasure up in our hearts the wonderful revelations given to us in God's Word? First, we should focus on the gospel: in one sense, of course, Jesus is the reason for the season. But in another fundamental sense, *sin* is the reason for the season. We have not entered into a season of feel-goodism, where we think about soft snow and candlelight, with silver bells in the distance. Remember Ramah weeping for her children, remember our abortion mills, remember how dark this world is without Christ, and then cling in faith to the death, burial, and resurrection of Jesus Christ. Mary's only Savior is our only hope for salvation as well.

Second, we need to connect this with strong views of incarnationalism. Not only has Jesus destroyed the overt works of the devil, He has also thrown down the devil's philosophy, which maintains that we are all to be very, very "spiritual." But in the face of this false doctrine, God was made *flesh*. This means that we may build, sew, pick up a knife and fork, make love, spank our kids, shovel the walk, and do all to the glory of God. Earthiness is not the gospel, but the gospel *did* come to earth. Earthiness is no savior, but earthiness is saved.

And last, we glory in victory: He came to make His blessings flow far as the curse is found. God did not give His Son to die in order to fight against the world with futility. The incarnation was no temporary arrangement. The baby born at Bethlehem was given as the Savior of the world.

We all enjoy the anticipation of each new Christmas, and we all rejoice in the celebrations. But we don't ever want this celebration to drift off point—this is not the armistice day of a long-forgotten war. This war is ongoing, and we celebrate this decisive point in the war as a means of continuing the faithful battle.

FALLING AND RISING

And, behold, there was a man in Jerusalem, whose name was Simeon; and the same man was just and devout, waiting for the consolation of Israel: and the Holy Ghost was upon him. And it was revealed unto him by the Holy Ghost, that he should not see death, before he had seen the Lord's Christ. And he came by the Spirit into the temple: and when the parents brought in the child Jesus, to do for him after the custom of the law, Then took he him up in his arms, and blessed God, and said, Lord, now lettest thou thy servant depart in peace, according to thy word: For mine eyes have seen thy salvation, Which thou hast prepared before the face of all people; A light to lighten the Gentiles, and the glory of thy people Israel. And Joseph and his mother marvelled at those things which were spoken of him. And Simeon blessed them, and said unto Mary his mother, Behold, this child is set for the fall and rising again of many in Israel; and for a sign which shall be spoken against; (Yea, a sword shall pierce through thy own soul also,) that the thoughts of many hearts may be revealed. (Lk. 2:25–35)

After the birth of Jesus, Joseph and Mary brought Jesus up to the Temple to do for Him what the law required (v. 27). There was a just and devout man there named Simeon, and the Holy Spirit was upon him (v. 25). He was waiting for the consolation of Israel, and it had been revealed to him that he would not die before he had seen this consolation, the Messiah Himself (vv. 25–26). The Spirit brought him into the Temple, and he came up to Joseph and Mary, took the baby in his arms, and blessed God (v. 28). His first word considered what God had promised to him (vv. 29–32), which is that he would see God's salvation, a light for the Gentiles and the glory of Israel (v. 32). Joseph and Mary were both amazed (v. 33). And his second word was a word of blessing for Joseph and Mary, and he turned and said something to Mary in particular (v. 34). Remember this is all in the context of a *blessing*. The child is set for the fall and rise of many in Israel, a sign that will be spoken against (v. 34). A sword will pierce through Mary's soul (v. 35), and the thoughts of many will be revealed (v. 35). The definition of history, which we will consider here, is all wrapped up in this blessing for Mary. There are four elements to this blessing, which we will consider in turn:

1. The fall and rise of many in Israel
2. A sign that will be spoken against
3. A soul-piercing grief for Mary
4. The thoughts of many revealed

First, history is a story. It unfolds and develops, and this means that the characters involved are going somewhere. The last chapter will differ from the first. Because this is a long story, this happens in cycles. Because of what Scripture teaches us throughout, there are only two ways for this to go. They are *fall and rise*, or *rise and fall*. It is either death, resurrection, and glory, or it is glory, pride, and death. And at each stage of this development, we have the setting for the alternative. If history were frozen, we could have static good guys and bad guys. But those who fall and rise might need to fall again. These things were written for us as an example, on whom the ends of the ages have come (1 Cor. 10:11). "Don't be that guy" in the story is a reminder that is constantly necessary. Pope Alexander VI should have been more interested in Caiaphas than he was. Yesterday's poor, now delivered, are tomorrow's wealthy, who therefore need to hear the warnings.

Second, Jesus is to be a "sign" that is spoken against. Signs carry meaning, and when someone speaks against such a sign they are saying, "No, that's not what it means." But when God gives a sign, He gives it with a meaning that is *plain*. The culmination of this sign was the resurrection of Jesus, by which He was declared to be the Son of God (Rom. 1:4). This divine Sonship means that Jesus will judge the world at the culmination of human history (Acts 17: 31), and that He is the prophet, priest and king over all things now (Ps. 2:8).

Third, grief is real. We have every reason to believe that Mary is among the witnesses of the resurrection (Acts 1:14). But she knew, long before this, that the supernatural had invaded our world. George Herbert has a poem where he plays on the letters in the words *Mary* and *Army*, and says that this was fitting, for it was there that God pitched his tent (Jn. 1:14). Mary knew she was a pregnant virgin, Mary knew what Simeon told them here in our text, she knew what the angel had said, and more. So she knew that the cross was not the end of the story—but it was true grief *in* the story nonetheless. Knowing we are in a story does not prevent real story grip from happening. A sword went straight through Mary's soul—and she knew that it was coming years in advance.

We have noted before that the weeping of Rachel for her children is part of the Christmas story. Nativity sets should have models of Herod's soldiers in them, and nativity sets ought *not* to have little drummer boys. This violence was part of the story. We should note also that Simeon included the violence that would be directed against Christ, and which Mary would feel in her soul, and he included this in the story from the very beginning. Earlier in the chapter, we read that Mary treasured up in her heart what the shepherds had said, and it says that she pondered them (v. 19). Luke tells us at the beginning of his gospel that he gathered his account of these things from eyewitnesses (1:2). Clearly, one of his chief sources was Mary. From whom did he find out about Simeon? Again, when Luke was writing, Mary was the only eyewitness of that event. And she clearly remembered what Simeon had told her. She was preparing herself for the crucifixion, in some measure, from the infancy of Jesus on. But she also knew that this prophetic word came to her in the context of a *blessing*.

Blessings have a story arc. Simeon said that there would be falling and rising. Blessings are not static. When Simeon told Mary about the pain that was coming, he had already said that the baby in his arms was the Lord's "salvation" (v. 30). Mary knew, from Simeon's mouth, that Jesus was the *Christ* (v. 26). Mary knew that this was a story that would not end in disaster. It would have a disaster *in* it, but not in the final chapter. The gospels are not tragedies in any sense. They are not comedies either, if we take comedy as referring to something humorous. They are comedies in a much deeper and more profound sense than this. Christ was born to die, but He died so that He could be the first born from among the dead (Col. 1:18).

And lastly, Christ's coming will reveal what is in our hearts. We want to keep the thoughts of our hearts bottled up. As long as they are there, deep inside, we may pretend that we are the lord of them. No one else knows our spites, our petty adulteries, our envyings. We keep them under our tongue like a sweet morsel. The doctrine of God's omniscience refutes this, but we have learned how to keep our doctrines up in the heavens. But Jesus—He has come down. He lived among us. His presence reveals, like nothing else can reveal, the thoughts and intents of our hearts. Not by projecting them onto a screen, but rather by showing the world whether we are drawn to Him, or repulsed by Him. From the moment Simeon spoke those fateful words, the winnowing has been in effect. *Come to Jesus*, or *go away*. In Him is light, and away from Him is only darkness.

FALLING AND RISING II

As we continue meditating on the meaning of Advent, we are not as much resisting attempts to make Christmas meaningless as we are fighting with alternative meanings. There is no such thing (in the last analysis) as a vacuum holiday, a celebration without a point. Attempts to neutralize Christmas are simply an intermediate step—and the alternative meanings are waiting in the wings.

> And Simeon blessed them, and said unto Mary his mother, Behold, this child is set for the fall and rising again of many in Israel; and for a sign which shall be spoken against; (Yea, a sword shall pierce through thy own soul also,) that the thoughts of many hearts may be revealed. (Lk. 2:34–35)

Simeon was a great man of faith, an Old Testament saint who was waiting faithfully for the consolation of Israel. By the grace of God, he was permitted to live long enough to see the Messiah as an infant. But he was not just a man of faith; he was given a prophetic word. Among other things, he blessed Joseph and Mary both (v. 34), and then turned to Mary and gave her a particular word. The child was destined to be a divider. On the one hand, he would bring about the fall and rising of many in Israel, which was a good thing (v. 34). On the other hand, he would be "for a sign" to be spoken against (v. 34). Not everyone would receive the Messiah with glad shouts of acclaim. Simeon hints that more than just speaking against Him would be involved, because he predicted that a sword would be run through Mary's soul (v. 35). This is a clear indication that Mary would live to see the crucifixion, which did happen (Jn. 19:26–27). The fact that Jesus would be for a sign to be spoken against was in order to reveal the condition of many hearts (v. 35).

What does it mean to say that alternative or competitive meanings for Christmas are positioning themselves? Usually the answer comes out when someone points to something that everyone is supposed to acknowledge as problematic, and says something like, "We have to get away from this problem or that one, and get back to the *true* meaning of Christmas." The fact that the problems are so obvious is used in a trick to make us think that the proposed meaning is self-evident also. What are some of those false solutions?

Sentimentalism—a sentimental Christmas is a Christmas without conflict. Sin brought conflict and violence into the world, and so in a very real sense, Christians are enemies to the way of death. But note this: death is our *enemy*. We cannot rid the world of conflict without conflict. But it must be the God-ordained kind of conflict, as Simeon foresaw. The pseudo-problem that people point to is the mere *existence* of conflict, never mind who is right or wrong.

Moralism—a moralistic Christmas is a Christmas without sin. People are changed (if they need to be changed) the way Scrooge is transformed in *A Christmas Carol*. They are changed by simply changing their minds, and giving somebody a goose or something equally festive. This kind of Pelagianism is *not* what we are commemorating. But Simeon's prophecy takes real sin into account. Note the prophetic language of judgment—falling and rising, a sign that is hated, a sword piercing the soul of a godly woman, and the revelation of many hearts. The pseudo-problem that is raised here is the problem of "negativity." But when Christ was born, our world was cold and black.

Spiritualism—a spiritualistic Christmas is a Christmas without matter. But when Simeon blesses Joseph and Mary, he is doing so because they are there in the Temple with a baby in their arms. The Lord was taken up in Simeon's *arms* (v. 28). Jesus was a baby, a material gift. We do not celebrate Christmas by trying to backpedal away from the world of material things. The pseudo-problem here is the warning against "materialism," as though matter were somehow inherently a problem. Idolatry is a problem, but *that* can occur with thoughts and virtual reality as easily as with fudge and presents. Remember that it was *Judas* who wondered why the precious ointment was poured on Christ's feet instead of being given to the poor. Another manifestation of this problem is the idea that Christ's advent was somehow apolitical. Herod didn't make this mistake—but more on that later.

So if we tell the Christmas story carefully, taking note of all the things that the writers of the scriptural accounts include, we find ourselves telling the entire story of salvation. The story includes the world, and everything in it. He came to make His blessings flow, far as the curse is found.

GOOD WILL TOWARD MEN

Grace is one of the most difficult things in the world for sinners to grasp. And as soon as we gather that it is difficult, we turn the "grasping of it" into a contest and a work, with the right answer earning the "best in show" award. But of course, grace means that some with the wrong answers will be saved and some with the right answers won't be. The salvation that came to the world was all of *grace*.

And there were in the same country shepherds abiding in the field, keeping watch over their flock by night. And, lo, the angel of the Lord came upon them, and the glory of the Lord shone round about them: and they were sore afraid. And the angel said unto them, Fear not: for, behold, I bring you good tidings of great joy, which shall be to all people. For unto you is born this day in the city of David a Saviour, which is Christ the Lord. And this shall be a sign unto you; Ye shall find the babe wrapped in swaddling clothes, lying in a manger. And suddenly there was with the angel a multitude of the heavenly host praising God, and saying, Glory to God in the highest, and on earth peace, good will toward men. (Lk. 2:8–14)

As we have all heard many times, there were shepherds in that area, watching their flocks by night (v. 8). But do not think of a quaint pastoral crowd—this was much more likely a group of tattooed roughnecks than anything else. Shepherds were not part of the upper strata of Israelite society. One angel appeared to them, and the glory of the Lord shone all around them, and they were terrified (v. 9). The chances are good that the angel interrupted them in the middle of a ribald joke. The angel told them *not* to be afraid—he brought them *good* news, tidings of *great* joy, and the message was for *all people* (v. 10). The basis for the joy was the fact that Christ the Lord had been born in Bethlehem that day (v. 11). A sign was given—the baby would be wrapped up, and lying in a manger (v. 12). After the angel of the Lord had finished saying this, this great message of *peace* was reinforced by a heavenly *army* (v. 13). The multitude (many thousands) said this (v. 13) in their praise of God: (1) Glory to God in the highest, (2) peace on earth, and (3) goodwill toward men. The difference between the AV and some other translations is a manuscript issue, not a translation debate, and for reasons that will become obvious soon, we will be continuing to follow the AV.

We have trouble with something as straightforward as "goodwill toward men." We are afraid of grace getting carried away, and so we want to slap some conditions on it. This shows up in some of the other readings. "Glory to God in the highest, And on earth peace among men with whom He is pleased" (Lk. 2:14, NASB). This is consistent with that peace being limited to about twenty-eight people—surely God cannot be pleased with any more than that. The goodwill and the peace are dispensed with a teaspoon within a select club, and we no longer have to worry about His apparent spendthrift ways.

But there are too many passages which make God's saving and gracious intention for the entire world clear and plain. So we ignore them, or move them to some trans-historical place. But we have to do something about the verses that frequently show up on Christmas cards. Surely, this doesn't "really mean" that God's goodwill is extended to all men *generally*? Yes, it does. First, quite apart from the manuscript issue, notice what the angel of the Lord had said before the whole heavenly army appeared and sang the chorus. He had said that this was "good tidings of great joy," and it was for "all people" (v. 10).

And grace spreads in a particular way. The fact that God has every intention of saving the entire world is a *gracious* message. And those who are worried about us getting carried away with talk of indiscriminate grace don't need to worry. Herod was not a messenger of this grace (although he was an unwitting instrument of it). False teachers are not messengers of this grace (although they too are encompassed by God's purposes). Grace has a backbone, and knows how to define itself. In part, that is what we need to be doing here. Grace is not the word that we are to use as the "open, sesame" of the Church. Grace is not something we *do*. Grace is not something we can *control*. Grace is not something we can *manage*. And this means that we in the Church, particularly in the *sola gratia* wing of the Reformed church, need to recognize that curators of grace are frequently the most dangerous enemies of grace. Grace is God's declared intention for the whole world, whether we like it or not.

The word used for *good will* in the famous phrase "good will towards men" is a cognate word to the expressions of pleasure that God pronounced over His Son. "This is my beloved Son, in whom I am *well pleased*" (Mt. 3:17). We are clearly not in this position of favor through any great moral achievement of ours— in the city of David was born a *Savior*. The Savior brought deliverance and forgiveness, which we in our sin desperately needed. We declare this, we preach it, we announce it, which is God's way of propagating it. And if God said to all mankind on that first Christmas night, "I don't care how rotten you have been . . . here, in the city of David, a Savior is born," how much more willing would He be to say this to you? "I don't care how rotten you've been. Got that? *I don't care.*"

We know our Bibles well enough to know that grace, properly understood, does not lead to a life of moral outrage. "What shall we say then? Shall we continue in sin, that grace may abound?" (Rom. 6:1). Of course not. We know the Scriptures in this, but I am afraid that we do not know our own hearts. God's grace is a tsunami that will carry us all away, and deposit us in places we would not have anticipated—and all of them good. We analyze all this carefully, and say that we want our grace to be genuine water, just like the tsunami, but we want it to be a placid pond on a summer day that we can inch across gingerly, always keeping one pointed toe on what we think is the sure bottom of our own do-gooding morality. As the old blues song has it, everyone wants to go to heaven, but nobody wants to *die*. Everyone wants to cross the Jordan, but nobody wants to swim.

So let's go back to the shepherds. God has declared, through His angelic emissaries, His *goodwill* toward our world. He has declared His intentions for *peace*. He did not do this so that we would then *drastically* restrict the message to a tiny club for peace and goodwill. The gospel is for the world. The reason we have trouble with this is that we think it means having the world fit into our tiny club. But they wouldn't fit, and they don't want to come. That won't fix anything. So God took unilateral action, and through His angels He made a unilateral declaration to some shepherds.

STAR OF BETHLEHEM

One of the most obvious symbols of the Christmas season is the star of Bethlehem. Countless Christmas cards have portrayed it, our carols sing about it, and we tell one another the story associated with it every year. In doing this, we frequently just skim over the surface of what we actually think we are saying. But can stars do what we all say this star did?

> And Balak's anger was kindled against Balaam, and he smote his hands together: and Balak said unto Balaam, I called thee to curse mine enemies, and, behold, thou hast altogether blessed them these three times . . . And now, behold, I go unto my people: come therefore, and I will advertise thee what this people shall do to thy people in the latter days. And he took up his parable, and said, Balaam the son of Beor hath said, and the man whose eyes are open hath said: He hath said, which heard the words of God, and knew the knowledge of the most High, which saw the vision of the Almighty, falling into a trance, but having his eyes open: I shall see him, but not now: I shall behold him, but not nigh: there shall come a Star out of Jacob, and a Sceptre shall rise out of Israel, and shall smite the corners of Moab, and destroy all the children of Sheth. (Num. 24:10–25)

Balak, king of Moab, had summoned the prophet Balaam to curse the Israelites who were massed on his border. Balaam was a true prophet, but he was not a true man. That is, he had a genuine prophetic gift, but he was a corrupt and sinful man. He could not speak prophetically against the spirit within him (Num. 24:12–13). At the same time, he was not above giving a little shrewd and godless counsel to the Midianites (Num. 31:16), urging them to seduce the Israelites into the cult of Baal-peor. In the New Testament, his name is associated with greed and avarice (2 Pet. 2:15; Jude 11), along with participation in licentious paganism (Rev. 2:14). When the Israelites invaded the land, he was justly killed (Num. 31:8).

So Balaam was a Gentile prophet, and we have no reason to suppose that his prophecy here could not have been preserved outside the scriptural record, and known to the magi from the East. What do they say when they arrive before Herod? They state they saw a star in the east, and they came to worship the one who was born king of the Jews (Mt. 2:2). Now Balaam's prophecy is very clear in its association of this star from Jacob with a coming messianic kingship. The star signifies a scepter. The magi were Gentile magicians or astrologers, and they came to worship the king of Jews.

The Scriptures do not describe a universe in which we are confronted with a "miracle a minute." Frequently false scriptures are marked by their error of thinking if "one's good, two's better." We might think of this as miracle inflation. But neither are we shown a blank, drab, and gray infidel universe either, where all we see is matter in motion. In Scripture, the miracles that occur can be staggering, and *if we think about it* there is no way to get our Enlightenment-trained minds around them. Some of the mind-blowing miracles are embedded in the story in such a way that we feel safe from them, at least until we make a point of thinking about them. Miracles like the Incarnation and resurrection are like this. But others are just right "out there," and you either believe the Bible or you don't. This might be called the

Enlightenment Assumptions Detector test (EAD). What do you do with Jesus walking on the surface of the water? And what do you do with the star of Bethlehem?

One evangelical Bible dictionary does this: "While full weight must be given to the poetic descriptions in the story (e.g., the star standing over Bethlehem), descriptive symbolism neither affirms nor negates the historicity of the event involved. A literalist approach, either to de-historicize the story or to exaggerate the miraculous, is out of keeping with the evangelist's meaning." This is done with a great deal of scholarly throat-clearing, of-coursing, and be-that-as-it-maying, but for all that, to the eyes of simple, biblical faith, his argument looks like a helicopter trying to land sideways.

But what *is* a star anyway? This kind of miracle is hard on modernists trying to be Christian because it is a miracle that depends on the universe being a very different kind of place than their modernist descriptions of it. If the narrative is to be trusted (and for evangelicals, it must be), then the star of Bethlehem identified a particular house in Bethlehem, singling it out from the others, in order that the magi would know what door to knock on. Now Bethlehem was only about six miles away from Jerusalem. Imagine trying to follow a star over to a town that far away from yours, and having it pick out a house for you. Now either the magi were doing some serious astrological math on the back of their camels (in the dark), or a star came down into our sky and stopped over a particular house, which is what the text explicitly says (Mt. 2:9). And "till it came and stood over where the young child was" is not a scriptural poetic phrase, meaning that the wise men really asked around in Bethlehem, and then looked up Joseph and Mary in the phone book. But giving offense to modernist cosmologies is not a sufficient criterion for establishing the presence of "poetry" or "dramatic symbolism."

So based on the *text*, we either have serious astrology or a physical star leading the way to a house. But in either case, a star cannot be what our modern cosmology demands we believe it to be. "'In our world,' said Eustace, 'a star is a huge ball of flaming gas.' 'Even in your world, my son, that is not what a star is but only what a star is made of.'"[1] Think for a moment about what a bizarre place the universe actually is, and how we moderns have tried to use our powers of imagination to tame it, instead of using our imaginations for the purpose that God gave them to us—to enable us to *see* it.

The unbelieving mind and heart looks around at the "given" world he sees, and just takes it as a *birthright norm*. This is the way things "just are" he boasts, and he is "a realist" for seeing it. If someone comes back from the other side of the world with some strange tales, then the traveler is laughed to scorn for his superstitious naiveté. But the failure of the modernist imagination can be seen starkly here. The hide-bound rationalist *cannot put himself in another place*, and he cannot conceive of his so-called normal world being described to creatures far off, and having them laugh at it as "way too bizarre to be real."

But we live in a universe in which we know you can discover things like giraffes, brussel sprouts, ankles with their superb engineering, rime frost, crab nebulae, volcanoes, toast, butter, buttered toast, a rhinoceros, toes, colors, musical harmony, oceans, whales, and Kentucky bluegrass. Not only can we not give an account of all this, but on our own autonomous footing, we cannot give an account of *any* of it.

Apart from the triune God of Scripture, we cannot know anything. If we believe in Him, we can know the world around us. But He is the Lord, and He might tell us of some other remarkable things he has done. He might tell us about the time He sent one of His celestial glories down into our sky over Bethlehem. And He did this to especially mark the most remarkable thing

1. C.S. Lewis, *The Voyage of the Dawn Treader* (New York: Harper-Collins, 1952), 209.

that He ever did—His eternal Word took the form of a baby boy. And the miracle in the sky above was *nothing* in comparison to the miracle in Mary's arms in the house below.

WE THREE KINGS

The story of the magi within the Christmas narrative is not a standalone event. In the narrative, we find a type of how all the rulers of this world will eventually come to kiss the Son.

> Now when Jesus was born in Bethlehem of Judaea in the days of Herod the king, behold, there came wise men from the east to Jerusalem, Saying, Where is he that is born King of the Jews? for we have seen his star in the east, and are come to worship him. When Herod the king had heard these things, he was troubled, and all Jerusalem with him . . . When they had heard the king, they departed; and, lo, the star, which they saw in the east, went before them, till it came and stood over where the young child was. When they saw the star, they rejoiced with exceeding great joy. And when they were come into the house, they saw the young child with Mary his mother, and fell down, and worshipped him: and when they had opened their treasures, they presented unto him gifts; gold, and frankincense, and myrrh. And being warned of God in a dream that they should not return to Herod, they departed into their own country another way. (Mt. 2:1–3, 9–12)

After the birth of Jesus in Bethlehem, certain wise men from the east appeared in Jerusalem (v. 1), and they were looking for Him (v. 2). They knew they were looking for the King of the Jews because they had seen His star in the east, and they intended to worship Him (v. 2). Herod heard about this and he was troubled, along with all Jerusalem (v. 3). After Herod gets some information from his rabbis, he deceitfully sends the wise men on their way. After they left Herod's presence, the star they had seen back home led them to the right house in Bethlehem (v. 9). Seeing the star gave them great joy (v. 10). They came to the house (not the stable) where they saw the young Jesus along with Mary, His mother (v. 11). From the age of the boys murdered by Herod, we can infer that the wise men arrived sometime within two years of Christ's birth. They fell down and worshiped Him, and presented their famous and costly gifts—gold, frankincense, and myrrh. We don't know there were three wise men, this is simply an inference from these three gifts. God warned the wise men in a dream, and so they went home by another route (v. 12).

Despite the carol, these men are not described as *kings*, but there are good reasons for treating them as members of the ruling aristocracy, as men who could decide to go to visit a king. First, in the Old Testament, this kind of person was frequently found at court (magi, wise men). Second, these men were dignitaries of sufficient rank to have their questions attract the attention of a king, and to be summoned to his court. Third, their gifts to the young Christ were kingly gifts—the kind of gift that kings would receive from princes. Fourth, the text draws attention to a comparison between their eagerness to worship Christ, and Herod's false willingness to do so. Fifth, not only did God want the reader of Matthew to know that a king was born in Bethlehem, God wanted *Herod* to know that a king had been born there. And He wanted him to know it on the kind of authority that he would accept.

So what is this story doing here? The clear intent is to show us that Christ is a king, and He is the kind of king who receives legitimate worship from nobles. This is a proleptic story, meaning that it is prophetic. If the toddler Jesus receives this kind of honor, what will He receive later? He receives hostility at the beginning (from Herod) and He receives prostrate worship from Gentile noblemen at the beginning. This is an *a fortiori* situation—which one will win out?

Paul says that God wants all kinds of men to be saved and to come to a knowledge of the truth (1 Tim. 2:4). This "all kinds of" includes kings and those in authority (1 Tim. 2:2). In this matter, Paul practiced what he preached. When he had opportunity to present the gospel to kings and rulers, he did so (Acts 26:28). Kings are told to kiss the Son, lest He be angry (Ps. 2:12). While we are to fear both God and the king (Prov. 24:21), the king is to fear God particularly (Deut. 17:18).

Sin being what it is, this is not something that kings like to do. The gospel being as powerful as it is, however, means that the kings of the earth *will* come. They all will bring their honor and glory into the Church (Rev. 21:24, 26). They will become nursing fathers to the Church (Is. 49:23), submitting themselves to the Church, and being discipled by the Church. The phrase "nursing fathers" can be misleading, making us think the Church is somehow subordinate to the State—which is the opposite of what the passage actually says. In the restoration of Israel's fortunes (that is the Church), what does it say? "And kings shall be thy nursing fathers [lit. nourishers], and their queens thy nursing mothers: they shall bow down to thee with their face toward the earth, and lick up the dust of thy feet; and thou shalt know that I am the LORD: for they shall not be ashamed that wait for me." The leaves on the tree of life are for the healing of the nations, and they cannot be applied without the nations *actually getting better* (Rev. 22:2).

There are two ways to give. One is an act of authority and the other is an act of submission. There are two ways to receive—and not surprisingly, one is an act of authority and the other is an act of submission. Telling the two of them apart is perfectly clear for the humble, and opaque to the proud. Were the wise men placing Jesus and Mary in their debt with these very expensive gifts? Or were they showing their indebtedness? When our federal government today cuts a check, are they exercising authority or showing submission? This is not a hard question.

This story right at the beginning of Christ's life shows us the pattern that we should expect and require. Christ will not receive (and His Church must not receive) any money whatever from the state unless it is accompanied by prostration before Christ and true worship of Him.

WORD MADE FLESH

We ought always to reflect on the profound reality of the Incarnation. Over the course of time, we have added a bunch of cultural traditions to the celebration of the Christmas season, which is absolutely fine, but at the same time we want to take care not to obscure anything central. So, enjoy the fudge, and the sleigh bells jingling, and bringing the woods into your living room . . . but enjoy it all for the right reason.

> In the beginning was the Word, and the Word was with God, and the Word was God . . . And the Word was made flesh, and dwelt among us, (and we beheld his glory, the glory as of the only begotten of the Father,) full of grace and truth. (Jn. 1:1,14)

John's gospel begins with the words *in the beginning*, deliberately echoing the first words of Genesis (Gen. 1:1). Just as God created the heavens and the earth, so in the arrival of Jesus, He was recreating the heavens and the earth (v. 1). In the beginning was the Word, and the Word was *with* God, and the Word *was* God. What does this mean? The *withness* is defined by the word *Word*. The Word was *with* God the Father in the way our words are *with* us. They are not the same. And yet, at the same time, our words reveal us and are to be identified with us. We are what we speak. Out of the abundance of the heart, a man speaks, and we are this way because God is the same way. Out of the abundance of His heart, He speaks. Now, this perfect Word, this Word that came from the Father without any degradation of meaning, this Word which was also to be identified with the Father, what did He do? He became *flesh*, John says, and dwelt among us (v. 14). Did this bring about degradation of meaning? No, John says—we *beheld* his glory (v. 14). What glory? The glory of the only begotten of the Father. What glory? A glory that was *full* of grace and truth.

In one sense, Jesus said that He was the only one who had seen the Father (Jn. 6:46). But in His famous encounter with Philip later in this gospel, Jesus also said, "Have I been so long time with you, and yet hast thou not known me, Philip? he that hath seen me hath seen the Father; and how sayest thou then, Shew us the Father?" (Jn. 14:8–9). Jesus says here that the Word of God is not perfectly spoken within the triune life of God only. God has spoken Himself into a very imperfect and broken world, and He has done so *perfectly*. What does this mean?

Man in his sinful condition does not want to be saved. That is part of what it means to be a sinner. This means that man wants, by various strategies, to put himself out of God's reach. Some want to do it arrogantly, like the modern atheist who says there is no God. Communication is not possible, and the problem or fault is on God's end. He is to blame for not existing. But others want to pretend to a kind of humility, and so they act as though the problem is with our hearing, and not with God's speaking. "Yes," they say, "God speaks perfectly, but we are finite, limited, and selfish. We cannot pretend to know what He has said to us because we can only hear imperfectly. Anyone who claims to have understood what He has said must be really arrogant."

This postmodern foolishness makes a great show of adjusting to limits, and refuses to consider the implications of the

Incarnation. As Francis Schaeffer put it in the great title of his book, *He is There and He is Not Silent*. Modernists and postmodernists both believe that anything that proceeds "downstream" from a source is necessarily a degradation. Only the source can be pure. But their problem is that they have forgotten that God is triune, and that His Word is the *express* image of His person (Heb. 1:3). This is not like a series of gnostic emanations, or a line of xerox copies, with each one getting progressively blurrier, or some version of the telephone game, where the message gets increasingly garbled. Away with all that! We are *Christians*.

What does the Word say? The Word is the Logos, and He is not the *om* of Eastern mysticism. He does not smudge everything. He *articulates* it; He speaks it. Our Lord encompasses and embodies and exhibits *everything* that words do—exclamations, sentences, poems, stories, parables, sermons, lectures, novels, whispered conversations, propositions, questions, and more poetry. God speaks, and we are called to *listen*.

We worship the Speaker, the Spoken, and the Interpretation. Our triune God is not one frozen word, eternally stuck. The conversation is everlasting, glorious, swift, and beyond all reckoning. If this conversation were water, do not think of an infinite static ocean, but rather of an infinite cascading waterfall. No top, no bottom, no sides, no back, no front—and falling with infinite swiftness. God the Father speaks all of it, and the Word is all that is spoken. But who could possibly understand any of this? The Holy Spirit is the Wisdom that understands the conversation, *all* of it. "But God hath revealed them unto us by his Spirit; for the Spirit searcheth all things, yea, the deep things of God" (1 Cor. 2:10).

Now, consider the nature of the miracle we celebrate at Christmas. Without losing *anything* "in the translation," God brought *this* conversation into *this* world, starting in the womb of a young Jewish woman. The Word (the Word we have been speaking of) became *flesh*, and all carnal philosophy and wisdom fall backwards, like the men who came to arrest the Lord.

ISRAEL DOES IT RIGHT

In the name of the Father, who sent His Son to occupy the womb of a virgin, rejoice. In the name of the Son who gladly went, sing and be glad. And in the name of the Spirit, who enabled that virgin to miraculously conceive, bow down and worship. May the Father, Son, and Holy Spirit bless you and your entire household in this season of Christmas.

The Lord Jesus taught us that if we wanted to enter the kingdom of heaven, we needed to be converted, and become like little children. Jesus was very plain about it. "And Jesus called a little child unto him, and set him in the midst of them, and said, Verily I say unto you, Except ye be converted, and become as little children, ye shall not enter into the kingdom of heaven" (Mt. 18:2–3).

This saying has been swept up into many different discussions and debates—including debates over infant baptism, or the appropriate manners for Christians to have in order to be considered pious. But, in spite of all our discussions, by the power of the Holy Spirit, countless individuals have still been born again to God, and brought into the kingdom of heaven in just the way our Lord describes here. At the same time, it is not often noted that in saying this, the Lord was giving us something very important to think about during our celebration of the Incarnation, a theme to meditate on during all our Christmas festivities.

In calling us to this, we need to take careful note of the fact that Jesus was not telling us to do something that He was unwilling to do Himself. We should see this as the very model of His particular kind of servant leadership. Jesus told us to become like little children. And what did He do in the Incarnation? *He became a little child.* The one, in short, who told us that we needed to be humbled, converted, and made like little children, was the same one who humbled Himself and took the form of a baby in the womb of a young maiden. Jesus told us to become like little children, but He did so as the one who had—in an utterly unique way—become a little child.

He, the eternal Word, the one who spoke the galaxies into existence, was willing to become a little baby boy who could do nothing with words except jabber, and in that jabbering, make glad his mother and earthly father. He, the source of all life and all nourishment for that life, was willing to be breastfed. He, the same one who had separated the night from the day, and had shaped the sun to rule the day, and the moon to rule the night, was willing to have his diapers changed for a year or so. It is not disrespectful to speak this way; for Christians, it is disrespectful *not* to. We believe in the Incarnation, in the Word made flesh. This is our glory; this is our salvation.

Jesus told us that in order to enter His kingdom, we would have to stoop. This is not surprising, because He was the one who stooped in a mystifying way in the creation of that kingdom. He *stooped*—the ultimate Word became a single cell, and then a cluster of cells, and then visibly a baby, although still less than a pound, and then a child who kicked his mother from inside, delighting her immeasurably. He became a little child, and then, years later, He told us to copy Him in this demeanor—to become little children.

We were told to clothe ourselves with humility and tender mercies. When Jesus told His disciples to follow Him, the cross is certainly in view. We are to take up the cross daily and follow Him. But we do not just follow Him to the cross—we must also follow Him to the manger. We must become little children. We must be born again—not understanding this as a Gnostic experience of being zapped by a mystic and numinous light—but rather because we are way too adult, too full of ourselves, and self-important. The new birth is the birth of humility. What do you have right after a birth, including the new birth? A baby, which is what we are invited to become. A little child.

Theologians like to distinguish things—which is their glory—but they are frequently tempted then to run headlong and separate what they have previously distinguished, which is their besetting temptation and sin. For example, we distinguish the obedience of Christ on the cross, suffering for the sins of the world, from the perfect obedience that He rendered to God throughout the course of His life. The former is distinguished by theologians and called the passive obedience of Christ. The latter is called His active obedience. This is fine, and actually most necessary, so long as we don't try to separate them. As well try to separate height from depth, or depth from breadth.

The atonement did not start when the first nail went in and then stop when the Lord breathed His last breath. The entire life of Christ was involved in our salvation, from His conception on. Indeed, the prophet Isaiah said that we were healed by His stripes, which were inflicted *before* the cross (Is. 53:5), and that by His *knowledge* He will justify many (Is. 53:11). The Lord's time on the cross cannot be detached from the rest of His sinless life, and it is theological folly to try.

The early father Irenaeus taught, with a great deal of shrewd wisdom, a doctrine of the atonement called *recapitulation.* The Lord Jesus grew up through every stage of human life, and did so in order to be obedient there in that station, and to bring redemption to His people there. This does not exclude the cross—it culminates in the cross, where Christ died as a perfect substitute for all His people. But neither is it limited to the cross. Jesus is the last Adam. He is the new Israel. His perfect sinless life was redemptive precisely because in that life Israel was finally doing it right.

Irenaeus refers to this as *recapitulation*. British theologian N.T. Wright calls the Lord's life work in this the *reconstitution* of Israel. Classic Reformed theology calls it the *active obedience* of Christ. What it means, simply, is *Christ for us*. In your salvation, you were not given a fraction of Christ, but rather were given all that He ever did.

Throughout the Old Testament, the people of God were constantly veering off. They consistently fell, again and again, into their long-established patterns of idolatry and disobedience. And yet, they were the people of God, which only made their apostasies more grievous. One could be forgiven if he read through the first part of the Bible wondering when the normal people might arrive.

But in the life of Jesus, Israel finally does it right, and He does it right on behalf of *all* Israel, all who are gathered into Him by faith. In Jesus, the human race lived and obeyed perfectly before God in a way that the first Adam did not. That obedience of the Lord's is imputed to us, given to us, bestowed upon us, reckoned as ours. In the life of Jesus, Israel finally stops doing it wrong. But not only did the new Israel do it right, but He finished His life by sacrificing Himself as the blood atonement for all the wickedness committed in the course of the previous failures of the imperfect Israel. So Jesus is the reconstituted humanity. He is the new world, the new creation refashioned in the new heavens and new earth. He is the reconstituted Israel.

So how did He set about doing this? He became a little child. And how do we go about remembering it? By faith, a faith that participates in His humility, and imitates it. And *this* is what we mean by Christmas.

Our Father and God, we entrust ourselves to You in the name of Jesus, asking You to continue to fashion in us a true childlike humility, through the power of the Holy Spirit. Please receive our worship in and through the obedience of our Lord Jesus. Amen.

Lesson Two

THE POLITICS OF CHRISTMAS

There is a vast difference between narrow partisanship and a broad political worldview. Many Christians, in their attempts to keep the former out of their spiritual lives, have also found themselves excluding the latter. This is a drastic mistake. In doing this, they have found themselves without a consistent biblical worldview at all—because all worldviews are inescapably political. If you are resolved to be apolitical, you are resolved to abandon the world, to write it off.

But when Jesus was born into this world, the very last thing He was doing was writing it off. His arrival, though it occurred in an out-of-the-way place, nevertheless attracted the attention of foreign dignitaries and a persecuting king. The first Christmas was a political event of the first order, and every Christmas celebration since that time has been part of those political reverberations and echoes. How so?

AN EIGHTH DAY

And the evening and the morning were the eighth day. We should not be surprised at the pattern of darkness and then light, a pattern which we see not only in the creation of the world, but also in the re-creation of all things.

> I Jesus have sent mine angel to testify unto you these things in the churches. I am the root and the offspring of David, and the bright and morning star. (Rev. 22:16)

A number of the events of the first Christmas occurred at night. The angels announced the good news to the shepherds as they watched their flocks by night (Lk. 2:18). The wise men followed the star to Jerusalem, and then to Bethlehem, which meant that they were observing it at night (Mt. 2:9). Joseph fled to Egypt with Mary and Jesus, and he did so at night (Mt. 2:14). And one of the most obvious things about Christmas, when we step back and look at it, is that the first Christmas happened in the *world's* dark night. Evening, then morning, the eighth day. It is not for nothing that our Christmas carols have picked up on this theme—"It came upon a midnight clear," "Wake, awake, for night is flying," "How lovely shines the morning star," "As the Light of light descendeth from the realms of endless day, that the pow'rs of hell may vanish as the darkness clears away," "Amid the cold of winter when half-spent was the night," and "Disperse the gloomy clouds of night, and death's dark shadows put to flight."

When the sun rises, it does not happen the way a light comes on in a room when you flip the switch. The sun rises slowly. First you do not know if anything has happened or not. It may be just as dark as it was a moment ago, but maybe not. And some time later, you notice that the eastern sky is not what it was. There is *some* kind of light there. The stars that have been visible all night begin to disappear. Soon there is just one left—the morning star, the planet Venus, the last indication that day is coming. The next event is for the sun to actually rise, for the day to come. Christ was born at night, and His arrival was the arrival of the morning star. Note John's language again: Christ is the root and offspring of David and He is the morning star. He is the one who was born at night, and His birth was the arrival of the morning star. It is important for us to allow Scripture to tell us what time it is. If you did not already know, you could not tell the difference between a pre-dawn darkness and a twilight gloaming. Is the sun going down or coming up?

Christ Himself is the Word of God, and yet you have the Word of God in Your hands. Christ Himself is the day star, the morning star, and yet Peter tells us that to take heed to Scripture is to have the day star arise in our hearts.

> We have also a more sure word of prophecy; whereunto ye do well that ye take heed, as unto a light that shineth in a dark place, until the day dawn, and the day star arise in your hearts: Knowing this first, that no prophecy of the scripture is of any private interpretation. For the prophecy came not in old time by the will of man: but holy men of God spake as they were moved by the Holy Ghost. (2 Pet. 1:19–21)

Jesus Christ is the light of the world. In the heart of every converted person, He is the light within, the day star in the heart. But whether men are converted or not, blind or not, He is the day star of the world, the rising sun of the entire world. He is the light of every man.

In him was life; and *the life was the light of men*. And *the light shineth in darkness*; and *the darkness comprehended [overcame] it not*. There was a man sent from God, whose name *was* John. The same came for a witness, to bear witness of the Light, that all men through him might believe. He was not that Light, but was sent to bear witness of that Light. That was *the true Light, which lighteth every man that cometh into the world*. (Jn. 1:4–9, emphasis mine)

We ought not to think that, when men are converted, they each become a little lamp, and if enough of them get converted, they will be able to form a consortium and pool their lamps to try to make a sun. The vision of the coming noontime glory does not depend at all on *us* trying to get some momentum up. The sun has risen, and it will continue to do what rising suns do. Of course, individual response is important, but it is equally important to note what the response is to. The sun has risen. Christ has come. He is the king. The light covers the world. A return to heathen midnight is an impossibility. Those who walk in darkness now are doing so in a world suffused with light. This is hard to do—you have to remain blind, or hide in root cellars. There are ways to stay out of the sunlight, but they are difficult to accomplish. Not only so, but as the day passes, they will get *increasingly* difficult.

> Again, a new commandment I write unto you, which thing is true in him and in you: *because the darkness is past, and the true light now shineth*. He that saith he is in the light, and hateth his brother, is in darkness even until now. He that loveth his brother abideth in the light, and there is none occasion of stumbling in him. But he that hateth his brother is in darkness, and walketh in darkness, and knoweth not whither he goeth, because that darkness hath blinded his eyes. (1 Jn. 1:8–11)

The task of evangelism, now that Christ has risen, is not so much to run around at night, poking our flashlights into corners and cellars. Rather, the task of evangelism is more like pulling back the curtains. "But all things that are reproved are made manifest by the light: for whatsoever doth make manifest is light. Wherefore he saith, Awake thou that sleepest, and arise from the dead, *and Christ shall give thee light*" (Eph. 5: 13–14). Get out of that bed! Christ will shine on you!

So the secularists don't like the first Christmas, and they certainly don't like the subsequent ones. What are they going to do? Pass a law? This would be worse than King Canute's acted out parable when he commanded the tide not to come in—this would be Congress passing a law commanding the sun not to shine on places where the First Amendment was in effect.

Such laws, such foolish resistance, can cause short-term grief. Think again of Herod and the little boys he slaughtered. But think also about how ineffectual it was. Did he stop the morning star from rising? Did he stop the day from coming? In the same way, we must know that the message of Christmas is not that we have to persuade anybody of anything. The message is far more good news declaration than it is argumentation.

MERRY CHRISTMAS AS INSURRECTION

On a number of different occasions, we have considered the importance of having our times and seasons defined in relation to Jesus Christ. The only alternative to this is to have them defined in reference to someone or something else, and this is obviously an unacceptable alternative to all faithful Christians. Jesus Christ really has been established as the king of all heaven and earth. Our federal building downtown has a stone embedded in the wall that tells us the building was put up in the administration of Richard Nixon, 1973. The dating of each Christmas, with each year attached, tells us the same kind of thing, which is that the new heavens and the new earth are under construction, and have been for just over two thousand years.

What does Scripture say?

> For unto us a child is born, unto us a son is given: and the government shall be upon his shoulder: and his name shall be called Wonderful, Counsellor, The mighty God, The everlasting Father, The Prince of Peace. Of the increase of his government and peace there shall be no end, upon the throne of David, and upon his kingdom, to order it, and to establish it with judgment and with justice from henceforth even for ever. The zeal of the LORD of hosts will perform this. (Is. 9:6–7)

There are many things to note in this glorious text, and it is proper that we are reminded of this passage on many Christmas cards. The message of Christmas is *politically incendiary*, when you think about it, and it is not for nothing that secularists are trying to get us to forget Jesus with their C.E. (Common Era) and B.C.E. (Before Common Era), and seasonal conifers instead of Christmas trees. Nice try, but we aren't buying any.

We were not given a Son who *aspired* to have the government be on His shoulder. The *result* of His coming was promised just as surely as His coming was, and that result was that the "government *shall be* upon his shoulder." According to the prophet, this government will be established in fact (as it was two thousand years ago), and the growth and increase of that government will necessarily be inexorable. "Of the increase of his government and peace *there shall be no end.*" His government will not be manifested all at once because the prophecy describes it as needing to be ordered and established with judgment and justice. But this *will* happen, and we have the assurance that God is *zealous* to accomplish this. And so this is Christmas—a cornerstone in the building of a new humanity, a new heaven and a new earth.

We must come to realize the importance of "insignificant" faithfulness. A moment's reflection should reveal that the new Christian calendar system was not instituted by Herod the Great just after the wise men got away, or by Caesar Augustus. So when did this happen? And who did it? Anyone who has read Herodotus knows that the Scythians were a rough bunch, a reputation that may be reflected in the New Testament (Col. 3:11). As N.T. Wright describes it, by the fifth century, there was a thriving Christian church in Scythia, and at that time there was a Scythian monk named Dennis. The ancient form of that name would have been Dionysius. Because that name was so common then, he took the nickname of *Exiguus* (meaning little). And so you are now introduced to Dennis the Insignificant who, as the providence of God would have it, was one of the most *significant* figures of church history. He moved to Rome around A.D. 500 and he was the one who proposed that the calendar system be changed to date from the birth of Jesus Christ.

In his calendar, the New Year was the twenty-fifth of March (the Feast of the Annunciation), ninth months before Christmas. After all, that is when the Incarnation *happened*. So for a thousand years, the Christian New Year was March 25, and it was not moved to January 1 until Pope Gregory XIII reformed the calendar once more in 1582. And of course, we now know that Jesus was born in 4 B.C. and not four years later. But the issue is *symbol*, not simple reenactment.

But there are effective symbols like this one, and there are failed symbols. Several centuries before Dionysius, the emperor Diocletian revealed himself as a serious megalomaniac by trying to change the dating system to count from the year *he* became emperor. The Jewish false Messiah, Simeon Bar-Kochba, did the same thing. The devotees of the French Revolution attempted the same trick, dating the events of the whole world from 1792. But of the increase of *His* government and peace there will be no end.

However, these clowns at least knew how important this issue is, which is more than we can say of many modern Christians. And the Anti-Christian Liberties Union (ACLU) knows that getting Christmas trees off public property is well worth fighting for.

This is why we as Christians have to learn that saying "merry Christmas" is an act of *insurrection*. How do we define our lives? More than this, how do we define our lives *as a people*? Far from retreating into a minimalist celebration or no celebration at all, we as Christians must take far greater advantage of the opportunity we have in all of this. Now the Lord Jesus *is* on His throne. And His government *will* continue to increase. But He works through instruments, and one of His central instruments for establishing His kingdom on earth is the *faith* of His people. Why is it that Christians shopping at Walmart are being reminded over the loudspeakers that, "He comes to make His blessings flow, far as the curse is found?" Why are *they* telling *us* this? It's *our* religion. Why don't we believe it? And if you believe it, then say merry Christmas to somebody.

BLESSING OF SIMEON

The Lord has brought us safely through another year, and we are grateful for the time He gives us to meditate on the meaning of His Word, born into our midst for the salvation of lost and sinful men. This is the true meaning of Christmas, in contrast with the false antithesis so often propounded, which is between commercialism and generosity. That is not the antithesis; the true contrast is between Christ and sin.

> And behold, there was a man in Jerusalem whose name was Simeon, and this man was just and devout, waiting for the Consolation of Israel, and the Holy Spirit was upon him. And it had been

revealed to him by the Holy Spirit that he would not see death before he had seen the Lord's Christ. So he came by the Spirit into the temple. And when the parents brought in the Child Jesus, to do for Him according to the custom of the law, he took Him up in his arms and blessed God and said: "Lord, now You are letting Your servant depart in peace, according to Your word; for my eyes have seen Your salvation which You have prepared before the face of all peoples, a light to bring revelation to the Gentiles, and the glory of Your people Israel." And Joseph and His mother marveled at those things which were spoken of Him. Then Simeon blessed them, and said to Mary His mother, "Behold, this Child is destined for the fall and rising of many in Israel, and for a sign which will be spoken against (yes, a sword will pierce through your own soul also), that the thoughts of many hearts may be revealed. (Lk. 2:25–35)

Other than this passage here, we know nothing about Simeon. But when his actions are considered carefully, we recognize that he must have been a truly remarkable man. What was his character like? Luke describes him here as just and devout. A just man, he kept God's law and was upright and righteous. A devout man, he was careful, pious, religious, and faithful.

We also know of his patience. He was waiting for something, the Consolation of Israel. Recall that just and devout Jews had been waiting for this Consolation for centuries. He was not righteous in the sense of mere "rule-keeping," he was righteous in the sense that his eye was on *the historical fulfillment of God's promises*.

We also learn here of his inspiration—Simeon was an "Old Testament saint," and Luke tells us plainly that the Holy Spirit was upon him. The Holy Spirit had revealed to him that he would not die until he had seen the Christ . . . the Consolation of Israel. In fulfillment of this, the Holy Spirit brought Simeon to the temple at this particular time. "Simeon, I have someone I want you to see."

Mary and Joseph came to the Temple in order to "do for" Jesus according to the law. When they arrived, Simeon came and picked up Jesus and blessed God. He says that he was now willing to die in peace, for he had been given a glimpse of the beginning of God's salvation. This was a salvation *prepared* beforehand—the arrival of the Messiah was not God's afterthought. Nor was it accomplished by God in a corner. This was prepared before the face of all people. And here we are, two thousand years later. We are still talking about the ramifications of this event.

Christ came as a light to the Gentiles—Simeon knows that this salvation was not for a small ethnic minority of the world. God loved the world, and brought His Son into the world, and sent Him to the cross for the *world*. The cross is not for Jews only, but also for the sins of the whole world.

Simeon knew that he held a glory to Israel in his arms—in the first century, only a remnant of Jews were saved. But only someone as blind to the Scriptures as the unbelieving Jews of the first century could fail to see that great glory was coming to ethnic Israel. And if their failure was blessing to the Gentile world, what will their eventual repentance be but life from the dead?

The message of Christmas is a mingled one. On the one hand (as we've touched on before), we are taught to see it in terms of a *blessing*. Simeon speaks of it this way—he *blesses* Joseph and Mary. At the same time, we acknowledge the piercing of the sword which came to Mary, and we see why. But how was such a piercing to be a blessing to Mary—to see, as she was to live to see, her Son flogged and crucified? Because *that crucifixion was her salvation* as much as it was yours, or mine. She was to live to see the basis for her sins being forgiven. In a sinful world, this means that many will rise and fall. Our Lord is the great divider, and was identified as such from His youth.

And the conclusion of the matter is this: the meaning of Christmas is that the thoughts of many will be revealed. This is what the judgment of God does, and this is what the gospel does in averting the judgment of God.

POLITICAL CHRISTMAS

The carnal, unbelieving mind always understands political rule in a particular way. The names may change—Pharaoh, Caesar, pope, or president-for-life—but the underlying realities are always the same. These realities have to do with tyranny and coercion, and the imposition of a right-handed power, the kind of power that is necessarily suspicious of biblical liberty. This is a carnal, political power that breaks the two greatest commandments—it does not love God, and it refuses to love its neighbor. This is what denial of human rights amounts to—a refusal to love.

"When Herod the king had heard these things, he was troubled, and all Jerusalem with him" (Mt. 2:3).

"Then Herod, when he had privily called the wise men, enquired of them diligently what time the star appeared" (Mt. 2:7).

"Then Herod, when he saw that he was mocked of the wise men, was exceeding wroth, and sent forth, and slew all the children that were in Bethlehem, and in all the coasts thereof, from two years old and under, according to the time which he had diligently enquired of the wise men" (Mt. 2:16).

Jesus taught us that the children of this age are often more shrewd than the children of light are. They are often more aware of the ramification of what we say we believe than we are. When Herod heard of a king of the Jews, and of a star in the east, and of the wise men's intent to worship Him, he was troubled by this (v. 3). And given his position and disposition, this was an entirely predictable and natural response. He was not imagining things. Second, Herod took the news that the magi brought seriously. He investigated their timeline (v. 7), and he did so diligently. The birth of Jesus was a threat to him, and to his kind of rule, and he knew it very well. The seriousness with which he took these omens can be measured by what he was willing to do about it—which was to have the young boys in Bethlehem and the surrounding areas slain (v. 16).

From the very start, from the very beginning, the life of Jesus presented a potent threat to the status quo. This threat was not the result of Herod's paranoia—Herod knew what many Christians do not. The birth of this child meant that the old way of ruling mankind was doomed. The transition from the old way of rule to the new way of rule was not going to be simple or easy, but it was going to happen. Of the increase of the Lord's government there would be no end. But whatever it meant, Herod knew that he was against it.

But there are all kinds of workarounds that we have come up with, workarounds that enable timid Christians to rush in to assuage Herod's fears. "There is no need to panic, no need to kill anybody, no need to do *that*." But when we try to allay Herod's fears by telling him, in effect, that Christ's kingdom is an ethereal, spiritual, floaty-kind-of-thing, the problem is that we are bearing false witness.

Jesus came into the world to save us from our sins, and our political sins are not exempt from this salvation. Why would our political sins (which frequently have been among our foulest sins) be excluded? Jesus came as a Savior of our race. If that race was beset with seventeen different terminal diseases, why would Jesus come down to heal just two of them? And why would He leave the very worst of them untouched? Too many Christians need to be reminded not to rob Christ of the greatness of His offered salvation.

Jesus lived a bookended life. When Jesus was born into this world, the attention of the existing rulers was drawn to that fact. The political leaders were told about it. A star appeared in the sky, and respected wise men came on a long journey and brought their news straight to the court. And when Jesus was condemned to die, He was condemned by the Roman governor, at the insistence of a mob stirred up by the national parliament of the Jews. The life of Jesus, from beginning to end, was a public life. He was born in poverty, but not in obscurity. Given the physical circumstances, it would only have been obscure if the God of heaven had not made a point of leaving the rulers without excuse.

We have said many times before that Jesus came to show us a new way of being human. But this is not a lesson that we must learn "down in our hearts," and nowhere else. No, humanity is what it is in the recesses of our hearts, and it is what it is in the public square. Mankind is what it is both within and without, inside and outside. If it is true that Jesus was born into this world to show us a new way of being human, this must necessarily include what we do in every place in which we find ourselves. This includes when we are alone, when we are in bed, when we are at the dinner table with our families, when we are out around town, and so forth. Of course it includes every aspect of our lives. But it also includes every aspect of everyone's life—from the lowest hired hand up to the CEO of the corporation, from the most obscure citizen up to the greatest political dignitaries. God wants all to be saved and to come to a knowledge of the truth, from the king on down. The transformation that Jesus has inaugurated is no partial thing.

And so your celebrations are all to be conducted in the name of Jesus, of course. He is the reason for the season. But more than this, He is the *Lord* of the season. He is the Lord of the season because He is the Lord of the earth. He did not come down here, He was not born on this earth, in order to work out a power-sharing arrangement with Caesar. So let your Christmas celebrations be joyful all the way down to the ground. But in order for it to be the right kind of joy, those celebrations should be one of the most political things that you do. It should be the sort of thing that carnal kings worry about.

CHRISTMAS AND THE PHILOSOPHERS

When Christ was born into the human race, He had come to rescue a race that was entirely lost. We were not entirely *forsaken*—because of His gracious intention for us—but we were entirely lost. This means that everything we had with us was lost too. When a hiker is lost in the woods, not only is *he* lost, but everything in his backpack is lost with him. We were lost in our economics, lost in our politics, lost in our art, lost in our culture, and lost in our philosophy. And contrary to the assumptions of many, it was *not* the case that we were all of us lost except for our philosophers. It is closer to the truth to say that our philosophers were the navigation party, and not one person in our ranks was more lost than they were. They were the ones who brought what they thought were the maps and compasses.

We know that the Scripture tells us that Christ came as the king of kings. He is the one who triumphed over the principalities and powers. He was the baby in a manger who was a threat to Herod on a throne. His way of peace answered all the men of blood. But it is too often missed that the infant arms of the baby Jesus threw down *every* form of secular philosophy—not through anything his arms did, but rather through just the fact of *being* the small human arms of the Almighty. He did not just deal with the powerful. He also humiliated the scribe, the wise man, the debater of this age. If you are going to rescue a lost race, one of the most important things you can do is deal with their know-it-alls who like being lost, just so long as they get to write books about it.

It is not surprising that different errors are addressed by different holidays in the church calendar. Good Friday answers Nietzsche, Easter answers Schopenhauer, the Ascension answers Hegel, and Pentecost answers Spinoza. But Christmas is the final answer to Plato and Kant, and in many ways it is the foundational answer to all the others. This the rudimentary answer, the cornerstone answer—one that every Christian who has ever been tempted to take secular philosophers seriously should take to heart. Protagoras once said that man is the measure of all things—which was the height of our stupidity and folly. The Incarnation says rather that *the* Man is the measure of all things. Christians who must affirm the latter must also deny the former, and we must do so merrily and with good cheer. We do this as we gain His everlasting hall.

In the beginning was the Word, and the Word was with God, and the Word was God. The word for Word here is *Logos*, and the first verses of John sounded ponderous enough to catch the attention of the sophisticated chin-strokers of that age. Heraclitus had played with the idea of the Logos, and since the philosophers of Mars Hill liked nothing better than to kick around the latest thing (Acts 17:21), these starting verses sounded obscure enough to be really promising. But this was before verse 14 wrecked the seminar. The absolute Truth, the one who fills all things (Eph. 1:23) condescended to a place where He would have to fill His diapers. This—to the refined and philosophical mind—was outrageous, impudent, and even blasphemous. The entire Greek world came crashing to the ground by verse 14, when it says that the Word became *flesh* and dwelt among us. The ultimate Truth suckled at His mother's breast, had ten fingers and ten toes, which His mother counted, and He then grew a bit older and went to Nazareth High. The universal became a particular, and did so without ceasing to be universal. The universal Truth has a hometown, and a mom, and is a scandal to the Greeks. He is also a scandal to Kantians and the postmodernists, and all for the same reason.

This is the final answer to Plato, as has been noted more than once. There is now true union between the heavenly reality and earthly reality, and by knowing Him we can know them both. But it needs to be emphasized over and over, again and again, that the Incarnation marked by Christmas is also the final and utter refutation of Kant, and all the philosophers indebted to him downstream. The Incarnation answers Kant the same way it answers Plato—the Word became *flesh*. It is also beyond ironic that Kant's name was *Immanuel* Kant and, as we should know, *Immanuel* means "God with us"—the very possibility Kant was most concerned to deny.

One of the central reasons why we can have a *merry* Christmas is that Christmas enables us to not take the philosophers seriously. Not only that, but it enables us to not take anybody seriously whose thought presupposes taking these philosophers seriously. We are talking about real freedom here. And lest anybody get huffy, I am not talking about abandoning the life of the mind. I am talking about the true foundation of the life of the mind, which is loving Jesus, whose birthday we are marking.

These are not just raw assertions; this is not a disgruntled former philosophy major doing some trash talking. What does the Scripture tell us?

> [He] hath in these last days spoken unto us by his Son, whom he hath appointed heir of all things, by whom also he made the worlds; Who *being the brightness of his glory, and the express image of his person,* and upholding all things by the word of his power, when he had by himself purged our sins, sat down on the right hand of the Majesty on high. (Heb. 1:2–3)

Christmas means that the one who made the worlds came into *this* world, and did so as the brightness of the Father's glory and the *express* image of His person. God is here, God is with us. Jesus told Philip that if they had seen Him, they had seen the *Father* (Jn. 14:9). The Word did not come into the world in order to be degraded and unrecognizable.

When the Word was made flesh, and dwelt among us, what happened? John tells us that we beheld His glory, the glory of the only begotten of the Father. What we beheld was full of grace and truth. When ultimate reality came into this world, we beheld the glory of that ultimate reality. When God the Speaker spoke what He had to say into this world, He did so through God the Spoken. And lest we hunt frantically for some self-justifying, philosophically-necessary ignorance, God has also given Himself at Pentecost through God the Interpretation (1 Cor. 2:10). God really is *with* us. Everything Kant pretended not to know, the entire *noumenal* realm, is right here, wrapped in swaddling clothes. Philosophers might not know it, but shepherds do.

> That which was from the beginning, which we have heard, which we have seen with our eyes, which we have looked upon, and our hands have handled, of the Word of life; (For the life was manifested, and we have seen it, and bear witness, and shew unto you that eternal life, which was with the Father, and was manifested unto us;) That which we have seen and heard declare we unto you, that ye also may have fellowship with us: and truly our fellowship is with the Father, and with his Son Jesus Christ. And these things write we unto you, that your joy may be full. (1 Jn. 1:1–4)

Life is simple, and Christmas is *merry*. Manifested means manifested, not hidden. Seen and heard means seen and heard, not invisible and silent. Declared means declared, not muffled. Written means written, and why? That your joy may be full—joy to the world, the Lord is *come*.

MERRY CHRISTMAS TO CHRISTOPHER

Christopher Hitchens once wrote a piece for *Slate*, in which he was *bah humbugging* away like crazy. I know, that's what he always did, but here he was more focused, and the subject was Christmas, which is where *bah humbugs* are more appropriately out of place. If you know what I mean. And the issue, of course, was not tinsel, or snow, or eggnog, but rather the place and role of a public religion like the Christian faith.

> The core objection, which I restate every December at about this time, is that for almost a whole month, the United States—a country constitutionally based on a separation between church and state—turns itself into the cultural and commercial equivalent of a one-party state.[1]

And of course, here is some genuine humbug. The United States Constitution does *not* mandate separation of church and state. The phrase "wall of separation" comes from a letter that Jefferson wrote to the Danbury Baptists, and that phrase has no constitutional authority or ground. It was Jefferson's opinion, which, when he was alive, he had a right to. What the Constitution actually mandates with regard to religion is two-fold: one, the non-establishment of a national church by an act of Congress, and two, non-interference with the free exercise of religion by Congress. Got that? No Church of the United States, comparable to the Church of Denmark, or the Church of England. When the Constitution was ratified, nine of the thirteen colonies had established state churches at the state level. There is no conflict if the national bird is different from the various state birds, or

1. Christopher Hitchens, "Tis the Season To Be Incredulous: The moral and aesthetic nightmare of Christmas," *Slate,* http://www.slate.com/articles/news_and_politics/fighting_words/2008/12/tis_the_season_to_be_incredulous.html (accessed 10/25/2012).

the national flower from the state flowers, and so on. But if one Christian denomination were privileged at the national level, this could and would lead to conflicts with the established churches at the state level. Prior to the War Between the States, the country was governed on true federalist principles, and all this made sense. But get this down. The Constitution prohibits establishing a national denomination and supporting it with tax money. It does not require every branch of civil government, down to the smallest municipalities, to ignore the nature and will of the triune God. Still less does it require them to pretend that Jesus Christ, by His birth in Bethlehem, did not actually come to establish a new humanity in His own person and work.

But Christopher complains anyway, and he did so in the year of our Lord, 2008. He did so on the threshold of the next year of our Lord: "If the totalitarians cannot bear to abandon their adoration of their various Dear Leaders, can they not at least arrange to hold their ceremonies in private?"[2]

Now I fully understand the request. Can you not arrange to take your faith indoors, and make it a private matter? Keep it away from the rest of us? And here is the answer—*no*. The star appeared in the sky to announce the birth of one who would hold a universal scepter, and such scepters are not held privately, or stored in closets. The angels appeared to the shepherds to announce peace on earth, good will toward men, and our sorry world's screaming need for peace is a very public matter indeed. When Christopher and I were traveling on our book tour, he wore a red poppy the entire time, in commemoration of Armistice Day. He was willing to remember the day when the civilized nations decided to stop slaughtering one another by the metric ton, but he refused to mark the birth of the Prince of Peace.

Jesus really is Lord, and whatever else that claim is, it is no private matter. It is either true or false. Being true as it is, we sing

2. Ibid.

about it in the public square. Why? Because He came to make His blessings flow far as the curse is found. Where does Christmas belong? Wherever the curse is, and it seems to me this means we should *start* with the public square.

Lesson Three

CELEBRATING CHRISTMAS LIKE A PURITAN

One of the most common caricatures of the Puritans is that they were a lot of ecclesiastical killjoys, and that if their eyes were any closer together, they would each be on the other side. And while it is true that some forms of this caricature did come into existence later in the history of the Reformation, it is manifestly not true of the genius of true Puritanism.

The kind of exuberant and incarnational joy that is being commended in this book, a joy grounded on the bedrock of God's intervention in our history through the Incarnation, is a joy that should appeal greatly to every true friend of the Puritans. But in order to understand how this is so, some basic distinctions have to be made. How so?

GOD REST YE MERRY, GENTLEMEN

Advent marks the beginning of the ecclesiastical year. Every time we approach yet another celebration of Christmas as a people, we need to recall how to celebrate such days as the people of God. If we are not careful, we will stumble—perhaps to the right and perhaps to the left.

> For the weapons of our warfare are not carnal, but mighty through God to the pulling down of strong holds; casting down imaginations, and every high thing that exalteth itself against the knowledge of God, and bringing into captivity every thought to the obedience of Christ. (2 Cor. 10:4–5)

As we seek to celebrate Christmas rightly, along with observing the entire year in a Christian fashion, some problems do arise. As Reformed believers, we have to proceed cautiously as we talk about any celebration of a Christian year.

For example, some appeal to the stance of some of our Puritan fathers on this question. Weren't they against it? Well, yes and no, and what exactly was it that they were against? The Puritans were certainly against ecclesiastical corruption. A certain man once thought it good to pour used dishwater into the wine set aside for a feast. The master of the feast saw this and threw out the wine. *He* was then accused of ruining the feast.

Much has been made of the Puritan opposition to Christmas, but more than a little bit of the problem was caused by *how*

Christmas used to be celebrated. George Gillespie, a Scot at the Westminster Assembly, quoted Perkins, an English Puritan, on this subject, saying that the "feast of Christ's nativity . . . is not spent in praising the name of God, but in rifling [*raffling*], dicing, carding, masking, mumming, and in all licentious liberty, for the most part, as though it were some heathen feast of Ceres or Bacchus."[1]

The problem was actually comparable to us objecting to the drunkenness and fornication at Mardi Gras, only to be told that we have a problem with the resurrection because Lent is the preparation for Easter, and Mardi Gras is the last blowout before surrendering things for Lent. One of the central reasons Puritans were opposed to it was because of all the immorality that was going on in the name of Jesus.

There was another matter also, that of binding the conscience. One of the great achievements of the Reformation was the doctrine of the liberty of conscience, *rightly understood*. On their own authority, men do not have the right to bind the conscience of another in areas not addressed by the Word of God (WCF xx/ii). What does this mean? The short form in this context is that there is a difference between holy days and holidays—and between both of them and civil "days off." If someone's conscience does not permit them to celebrate any day like Christmas, we should be sensitive to that. Feeling sorry for their captivity to overdone scruples is one thing. But binding them, making them observe the day, or pressuring them to do so, is not permissible.

But the way I have construed this, the weaker brother is the one who does not observe Christmas. How do we answer the charge that it is actually the other way around, and that the "observer" is one who is guilty of syncretism? This charge of syncretism is often made—the Christian year is thought to be the

1. See George Gillespie, *English Popish Ceremonies* (Dallas: Naphtali Press, 1993), 340.

residue of long-forgotten compromises with paganism. And in its overgrown and encrusted forms this was frequently the case.

But in certain notable instances, the reverse was true. For one great example, according to the story, the Christmas wreath custom did not come from paganism, but from a remarkable *defeat* of paganism. Boniface (A.D. 680–754), missionary to the Germans, had chopped down a great oak, sacred to Thor. Three days later, on the first Sunday of Advent, he prevented a human sacrifice and used the sacrificial knife of the Druid priest to cut fir boughs for the people to take home as a reminder of Calvary. And for a second example, the inventor of Christmas tree lights (non-electric) was Martin Luther. This is because Jesus is the light of the world.

When it comes to holy days, and a Christian year, there *are* excesses to be guarded against. By the time of the Reformation the mentality of "if one's good, two's better" had taken over completely, and you couldn't swing a cat without hitting some saint's day or other. Confronted with this barnacle-encrusted church year, the Continental Reformers decided that the great points of the Gospel should still be celebrated, along with the rest of Christendom, but without getting entangled in a church year that was, honestly, over the top. Their "five evangelical" feast days were: Christmas, Good Friday, Easter, Ascension, and Pentecost. Or, if you wish, Good Friday and Easter could be considered as one holiday, and Trinity Sunday added.

Even the English theologians at Westminster (who took a harder line than those on the Continent) saw that it was lawful for the church to establish days for "thanksgiving upon special occasions" (WCF xxi/v). The text they cited for this was Esther 9:22, which records the establishment of Purim, a Jewish festival not required by the law of Moses, and which was an *annual* recurring celebration. And so in this spirit we might want to add Thanksgiving and Reformation Sunday to our calendars.

We will define our time by some system. The year is an inescapable year. Who is the Lord over it? How do we mark our days? Because we live in time, the rhythms of that time will either be Christian or not. To reject the one is to embrace the other. Because Christians no longer honor the Lord's Day on a weekly basis, the world has rushed to fill it with a frenetic 24-7 lifestyle woven around five days of work and two days of leisure. This is a marked difference from the one Christian day of rest, followed by six of work.

In the same way, because we have not seen the passage of the year under the lordship of Christ, we now find ourselves marking time with dates like Labor Day, Memorial Day, the Fourth of July, MLK Day, and so forth. But Christians must define the year in an explicitly Christian way, and face the objections, or they must acquiesce in the secularization of time. How then shall we live? We should leave our overly scrupulous brother alone. If God did not *command* something, then neither should we. We should walk in holiness, and not by corrupt behavior slander those holy days we are pretending to honor. And underneath it all, we should celebrate Christmas, and the rest of the church year, with a free (and clean) conscience. God rest ye merry, gentlemen.

PENITENTIAL SEASONS

As the church year developed in the medieval period, two great penitential seasons evolved. One was Lent, the preparation season for the celebration of Easter. The second was Advent, the run-up to Christmas.

As we are trying to orient ourselves by and with a Christian year, instead of the secularized civic year, we are certainly taking a step in the right direction. But this does not mean that there are no pitfalls as we move back in this direction of Christmas celebration. Secularism is the not the only spiritual danger facing us. We have to remember that the Church has been here before, and we have stumbled before.

If we want direction on how to observe a calendar year that is honoring to God, one of the places we should go is to the Old Testament. After all, all of Scripture is profitable for us as we are seeking direction.

And the LORD spake unto Moses, saying, Speak unto the children of Israel, saying, In the seventh month, in the first day of the month, shall ye have a sabbath, a memorial of blowing of trumpets, an holy convocation. Ye shall do no servile work therein: but ye shall offer an offering made by fire unto the LORD. And the LORD spake unto Moses, saying, Also on the tenth day of this seventh month there shall be a day of atonement: it shall be an holy convocation unto you; and ye shall afflict your souls, and offer an offering made by fire unto the LORD. (Lev. 23:23–27)

In Leviticus 23, the Lord revealed the great festivals of Israel to Moses. The weekly sabbath was first (v. 3). The other feasts (Passover/Unleavened Bread, Pentecost, and Tabernacles) were all *celebratory* in nature—they were feasts. And in our text above, we come to the singular Day of Atonement. On this day, the Israelites were commanded to "afflict their souls." God required this of Moses (v. 23). The day was set aside as a holy convocation, as a high sabbath, and was marked on a particular day (v. 24). Work was proscribed, as on a regular sabbath, and an offering of fire was required (v. 25). The Lord speaks again (v. 26), and He required the Israelites to afflict their souls (v. 27). There were other times of fasting, obviously, but these appear to have been occasional or individual. In the liturgical calendar of Israel, before the advent of the Messiah, one day out of 365 was set apart for the nation to afflict their souls. The rest of the commemorations were gratitude-soaked and celebratory.

In the early Church, celebration of the resurrection was instantaneous. From the very beginning, Christians celebrated and worshiped God on a weekly basis, and they did so by moving their observance from the seventh-day sabbath of the Jews to the first day of the week, the Lord's Day. This was done because this was the day on which the Lord rose from the dead. "Now when Jesus was risen early *the first day of the week*, he appeared first" (Mk. 16:9; cf. Mt. 28:1; Lk. 24:1; Jn. 20:19). From the pages of the New Testament down to the present, Christians have been observing the first day of the week as a weekly "Easter." "And *upon the first day of the week*, when the disciples came together to break bread, Paul preached unto them" (Acts 20:7). "*Upon the first day of the week* let every one of you lay by him in store, as God hath prospered him, that there be no gatherings when I come" (1 Cor. 16:2). "I was in the Spirit *on the Lord's day*, and heard behind me a great voice, as of a trumpet" (Rev. 1:10).

There are two striking meanings of this new day, this Day that the Lord has made. The first is the obvious meaning, which is that it marks the day of the resurrection. The Lord came back from the dead on the first day of the week (Mk. 16:9), appeared to His disciples on that same day (Jn. 20:19), and then appeared to them *again* on the following Sunday (Jn. 20:26). But what is the second meaning?

This second meaning is that God has recreated the heavens and earth. In the old covenant, the seventh-day sabbath was anchored to the old creation in an everlasting way. That seventh-day observance *was clearly going to last just as long as that created order did.* Nothing would suffice to change that day unless it were a change of the created order, unless it were the establishment of a *new* created order. And this is just what we find. "There remaineth therefore a [sabbath] rest to the people of God. For he that is entered into his rest, he also hath ceased from his own works, as God did from his" (Heb. 4:9–10).

Lent began as a period of preparation for Christian baptism—many of the baptisms in the early Church were performed on Easter Day. Over time, as an ungodly system of works-righteousness began to establish a deeper hold on the minds and hearts of many professing Christians, the church calendar began to reflect a false understanding of the nature of the gospel—as though holiness consisted of giving up things. Now we want to return to an explicit and Christian understanding of our days and years, which they certainly had, but we want to do this without making the same mistakes they did.

Traditionally, both Lent and Advent are penitential seasons—not times of overflowing celebrations. This is not something we have sought to cultivate at all, even though we do observe a basic church calendar, made up of what the Reformers called the five evangelical feast days. Our reluctance to adopt this kind of penitential approach to these seasons of the year is not caused by ignorance of the practice. It is a deliberate attempt to lean in the other direction. I want to present three arguments for a rejection of this practice of extended penitential observance.

First, if we were to adopt this practice, we would be in worse shape than our Old Covenant brethren, who had to afflict their souls only one day out of the year. Why would the time of *anticipation* of salvation be so liturgically celebratory, while the times of *fulfilled* salvation be so liturgically glum? Instead of establishing a sense of longing, it will tend to do the reverse.

Second, each penitential season keeps getting interrupted with our weekly Easters. Many who relate exciting movies they have seen to others are careful to avoid "spoilers." Well, these feasts we have, according to God's ordinance every seven days, spoil the penitential mood.

And last, what gospel is implicitly preached by the practice of drawing out the process of repentance and forgiveness? It is a false gospel. Now I am not saying that fellow Christians who observe their church year in this way are preaching a false gospel, but I am saying that *lex orandi lex credendi*—the law of prayer is the law of faith, and over time, this liturgical practice will speak very loudly to our descendants. If we have the opportunity to speak to our descendants, and we do, then I want to tell them that the *joy* of the Lord is our strength.

So as we prepare our hearts and minds, along with our families, for the annual celebration of our Lord's resurrection next Lord's Day, one other comment should be made. The Incarnation was a glorious event, and we don't want any diminution of that celebration. But the resurrection of the Lord was what remade the cosmos, and we should strive over time to have our celebration of Easter far surpass the glory of Christmas. We are currently more than a little lopsided—and we shouldn't try to fix this by reducing what we do at Christmas.

TWO KINDS OF SORROW

When we consider Isaiah 40, we see that there are two kinds of waiting. There is a waiting that causes our strength to dissipate, and there is a waiting that gathers our strength for us. There is a waiting that renews—an anticipation that is full of joy—and there is a waiting that is an emotional corrosive. I want to develop this idea further.

> Comfort ye, comfort ye my people, saith your God. Speak ye comfortably to Jerusalem, and cry unto her, that her warfare is accomplished, that her iniquity is pardoned: for she hath received of the LORD's hand double for all her sins. The voice of him that crieth in the wilderness, Prepare ye the way of the LORD, make straight in the desert a highway for our God. Every valley shall be exalted, and every mountain and hill shall be made low: and the crooked shall be made straight, and the rough places plain: And

the glory of the LORD shall be revealed, and all flesh shall see it together: for the mouth of the LORD hath spoken it. The voice said, Cry. And he said, What shall I cry? All flesh is grass, and all the goodliness thereof is as the flower of the field: The grass withereth, the flower fadeth: because the spirit of the LORD bloweth upon it: surely the people is grass. The grass withereth, the flower fadeth: but the word of our God shall stand for ever. (Is. 40:1–8)

The text begins with comfort (v. 1). Godly preparation does not begin with affliction, but such preparation actually *ends* the affliction. How so? The prophet speaks comfortably to Jerusalem, telling her that her sins are forgiven before the great deliverance arrives (v. 2). The next verse is a prophecy of the ministry of John the Baptist (v. 3; Mt. 3:3; Mk. 1:3; Jn. 1:23), who prepared the way for the coming Christ. Every valley is lifted up, and the high places are humbled—for just one example, Zebulun is humbled, and Galilee is exalted (Is. 9:1). Notice that this time of preparation is a time when things are made level, not uneven, when things are made smooth, not rough, when things are made straight, not crooked (v. 4). This time is aiming for a particular result, which is the revelation of the glory of the Lord, which all mankind will see (v. 5; Lk. 3:4–6). The prophet is told to cry out—but what is he told to cry? Men are like the grass, and their glory is like the flowers of the field (v. 6)—and as the grass withers and the flowers fades, so men also fade (because of the breath of the Lord). This passage is quoted by the apostle Peter (1 Pet. 1:24–25), to the effect that the Word preached to Christians is the Word that stands forever, and it is the Word by which Christians are born again (1 Pet. 1:23). This means that men who are regenerate are no longer numbered with the withered grass and fading flowers. That Word is preached "by the Holy Spirit" (1 Pet. 1:12), which is of course the same breath that makes the flowers fade.

Just as there are two kinds of waiting, so also there are two kinds of sorrow—and they parallel the two kinds of waiting. One dissipates strength and the other restores it. One kind of sorrow rakes you over the coals, and the other is the word that speaks comfort. "For godly sorrow worketh repentance to salvation not to be repented of: but the sorrow of the world worketh death" (2 Cor. 7:10). One sorrow leads to comfort and no regret, and the other leads to sorrow upon sorrow. You can be sorry today, sorry tomorrow, and you can die sorry. *That is not what Christ came to do for you.*

Our English words *repentance* and *penitence* are obviously related to one another (via the Latin *paenitere*), and we do have to be careful not to be superstitious about words. But there are different connotations to these words (in English) having to do with their history in our theological debates. Beginning with Tyndale, who translated the Greek *metanoeiete* as *repent*, instead of *do penance*, we have had a long history of distinguishing what it means to receive the grace of God, and what it means to try to surreptitiously earn the grace of God. Luther's 95 Theses began with this whole issue of penitence understood in gospel terms: "Our Lord and Master Jesus Christ, in saying 'Repent ye,' etc., intended that the whole life of believers should be penitence." True repentance should take the time to confess and forsake real *sin*, and the time should not be wasted through indulgence in nebulous angst about possible sinfulness that is always carefully undefined.

"Penitential" seasons can be put to a genuinely good use if they are a time when serious, once-for-all mortification of particular sins occurs—if real sins and real bad habits are uprooted from your life. Pray, practice, and pursue Colossians 3:5 and 3:8. Who could possibly be against that? The real problems come in when sin is not really dealt with, and yet the times of squirrel-cage-run penitence don't even slow down, and the penitent daily come to resemble more closely the policemen in *Penzance:* "Yes, but you don't go!"

Jesus assumes that such times can be spiritually healthy, but He requires His followers to keep it a secret that they are observing such a time.

> Moreover when ye fast, be not, as the hypocrites, of a sad countenance: for they disfigure their faces, that they may appear unto men to fast. Verily I say unto you, They have their reward. But thou, when thou fastest, anoint thine head, and wash thy face; That thou appear not unto men to fast, but unto thy Father which is in secret: and thy Father, which seeth in secret, shall reward thee openly. (Mt. 6:16–18)

A fast is a time for reflection, personal discipline, and confession, and if you are doing this during a penitential season, Jesus requires that you take reasonable measures to hide what you are doing from others. Why? Because your life should embody the truth that this entire season is a time when we are bringing to the world tidings of comfort and joy.

CHRISTMAS LIKE A PURITAN

Socrates once famously said that the unexamined life is not worth living. In a similar vein, the unexamined holiday is not worth celebrating. Whenever we do anything on autopilot, it is not surprising that at some point we forget where we are going, or what we were supposed to be doing. And when we are just cruising in a mindless tradition, it is a short time before sin takes over.

> And in this mountain shall the LORD of hosts make unto all people a feast of fat things, a feast of wines on the lees, of fat things full of marrow, of wines on the lees well refined. And he will destroy in this mountain the face of the covering cast over all people, and the vail that is spread over all nations. He will swallow up death in victory; and the Lord GOD will wipe away tears from off

all faces; and the rebuke of his people shall he take away from off all the earth: for the LORD hath spoken it. (Is. 25:6–8)

As the prophet Isaiah prophesies the coming of the new covenant, he does so with the image of a glorious feast. The feast is prepared by the Lord of hosts Himself (v. 6). What kind of feast is it? He prepares a feast of fat things, he prepares a feast of aged wines, of meat full of marrow fat, and then some more aged wines. *This* is the picture we are given of the gospel—not a glass of room-temperature water and a cracker. Right alongside this feast, in conjunction with it, He will remove the covering that kept us all in darkness for all those centuries. He will take away the veil over the nations (v. 7). The resurrection will come—and we have the down payment of *that* in the resurrection of Jesus— and death will be swallowed up in victory. The Lord will wipe away every tear, and all things will then be put right (v. 8). As those who have accepted this gospel, we have accepted that all of this has now been established in principle, and as we live it out in true evangelical faith, we proclaim this good news. But there must be continuity between what we are *saying* and how we are *living*. And by this, I mean much more than that our words should be true and our behavior good. I mean that our words should sound like good news and our lives should smell like good news.

Some of you have heard that the Puritans hated Christmas, that they were the original scrooges and grinches. But this, as is often the case, is grossly unfair to them. One of the Scottish commissioners to the Westminster Assembly, George Gillespie, a staunch opponent of the church year being used to bind the conscience, said this: "The keeping of some festival days is set up instead of the thankful commemoration of God's inestimable benefits, howbeit the festivity of Christmas has hitherto served more to Bachanalian lasciviousness than to the remembrance of the birth of Christ." In other words, a person might object to pepper spraying fellow shoppers on Black Friday without rejecting the blessing of Thanksgiving. He can object to a Mardi Gras orgy without objecting to the celebration of Christ's resurrection. He can turn away from a drunken office party without denying the Incarnation. And there was, for the Puritans, the matter of compulsion also.

Remember the words of C.S. Lewis here:

> There is no understanding the period of the Reformation in England until we have grasped the fact that the quarrel between the Puritans and the Papists was not primarily a quarrel between rigorism and indulgence, and that, in so far as it was, the rigorism was on the Roman side. On many questions, and specially in their view of the marriage bed, the Puritans were the indulgent party; if we may without disrespect so use the name of a great Roman Catholic, a great writer, and a great man, they were much more Chestertonian than their adversaries.[2]

This period of Advent is one of preparation for Christmas. If we want to celebrate Christmas like Puritans (for that is actually what we are), this means that we should prepare for it in the same way. Look at the whole thing sideways, like Chesterton would. Here are some key principles:

Do *not* treat this as a time of introspective penitence. To the extent you must clean up, do it with the attitude of someone showering and changing clothes, getting ready for the best banquet you have ever been to. This does not include three weeks of meditating on how you are not worthy to go to banquets. Of *course* you are not. Haven't you heard of *grace*?

Celebrate the stuff. Use fudge and eggnog and wine and roast beef. Use presents and wrapping paper. Embedded in many of the common complaints you hear about the holidays (consumerism,

---

2. C.S. Lewis, *Selected Literary Essays* (Cambridge: Cambridge University Press, 1969), 116.

shopping, gluttony, etc.) are false assumptions about the point of the celebration. You do not prepare for a real celebration of the Incarnation through thirty days of Advent Gnosticism.

At the same time, remembering your Puritan fathers, you must hate the sin while loving the stuff. Sin is not resident in the stuff. Sin is found in the human heart—in the hearts of both true gluttons and true scrooges—both those who drink much wine and those who drink much prune juice. If you are called up to the front of the class, and you get the problem all wrong, it would be bad form to blame the blackboard. That is just where you registered your error. In the same way, we register our sin on the stuff. But—because Jesus was born in this material world, that is where we register our piety as well. If your godliness won't imprint on fudge, then it is not true godliness.

Some may be disturbed by this. It seems a little out of control, as though I am urging you to "go overboard." But of *course* I am urging you to go overboard. Think about it—when this world was "in sin and error pining," did God give us a teaspoon of grace to make our dungeon a tad more pleasant? No. He went *overboard*.

A BRIEF HISTORY OF CHRISTMAS

We celebrate the birth of Christ, and we are able to do this because we have seen what His rule has accomplished in the world. Jesus told Thomas once that there was a blessing for those who would believe without having seen the risen Christ, as Thomas had (Jn. 20:29). On this principle, our place in history gives us access to a greater blessing because we have not seen Christ with our eyes. But it goes the other way also. Those at the time of Christ had not yet seen what His rule would do in history (as we have). And so they are more greatly blessed looking toward the future—the same way that we will be blessed by looking forward to what Christ has yet to do (1 Cor. 2:9).

> For unto us a child is born, unto us a son is given: and the government shall be upon his shoulder: and his name shall be called Wonderful, Counsellor, The mighty God, The everlasting Father, The Prince of Peace. Of the increase of his government and peace there shall be no end, upon the throne of David, and upon his kingdom, to order it, and to establish it with judgment and with justice from henceforth even for ever. The zeal of the LORD of hosts will perform this. (Is. 9:6–7)

There are many lessons that can be drawn from a rich text like this, but our task here will be to consider just two of them. The first is the Christmas element—the fact that a child is *born* unto us, and that a son is *given* unto us (v. 6). The second has to do with this child's relationship to what is here called "government." We are told that this child was born in order to *rule*, for the government will be upon his shoulder. And the second thing we are told about His government is that it will continually increase (v. 7). He will bear the government upon His shoulder, and it will be a continually increasing government. This increase—unlike the growth of secular governments—will be a blessing, and not a pestilence. This is the *real* big government.

The fact that Jesus was born into this world (*unto us*, it says) tells us that He is Lord of all things. He is the Lord of the earth. Further than this, after He rose from the dead and ascended into Heaven, He was given rule and authority over all things in Heaven and on earth (Mt. 28:18–20). And the fact that we are told that His government will steadily increase, without ever stopping, tells us that He is the Lord of time, the Lord of all history. He is Lord of the entire process. This includes those earlier times in the process when "the increase of His government" was not yet as obvious as it is now. This means that celebrations of

His rule will contain corruptions that need to be weeded out. The kingdom grows gradually, and problems are addressed gradually. But patience is a virtue. Jesus is the Lord of it all.

The early church celebrated what we call Easter (and others, *Pascha*) right away. This included the weekly "Easter" of the Lord's Day (Heb. 4:10; Rev. 1:10). One of the biggest controversies of the second century concerned how the date of this annual Easter was to be calculated. So the early church celebrated the Lord's resurrection (His being firstborn from the dead) from the very beginning. They were a bit slower with celebrating His birth. But given the amount of space the gospel writers gave to accounts of His birth, it is not surprising that this celebration came eventually.

The birth of the Lord began to be commemorated (on an annual basis) somewhere in the third or fourth centuries A.D. It is commonly argued that this was a "takeover" of a pagan holiday, celebrating the winter solstice. But it just as likely, in my view, that this was actually the other way around. *Sol Invictus* was established as a holiday by Aurelian in A.D. 274, when the Christians were already a major force. So who was copying whom? And Saturnalia, another popular candidate suggested as being an "ancestor" of Christmas, actually occurred on December 17.

St. Nicholas, who was later morphed into Santa Claus, was a godly man, known for his generosity to children. He attended the Council of Nicea (A.D. 325), and at least one urban legend has him punching out Arius the heretic. Let us hope so.

In the medieval period, in the eleventh century, the holiday became known by its current name (Christmas). *The Anglo-Saxon Chronicle* gives us the first use, recording something that happened in A.D. 1038. An archbishop died "and a little after, Ethelric, bishop in Sussex, and then before Christmas, Briteagus. Bishop in Worcestshire."

Some may object to the fact that the suffix -*mass* is still in the name. But the objectionable doctrine of transubstantiation was not codified by the Roman church until the thirteenth century (A.D. 1215) at the Fourth Lateran Council. The word *mass* originally came from the fact that in the ancient church catechumens were dismissed from the service before the Lord's Supper was observed. *"Ite, missa est,"* which roughly translated means that "you may go now." We see it still in our word *dismissed.* The vestigial reference to the Mass in this name should not be a trouble; Jehovah's Witnesses refuse to celebrate Christmas at all, and they deny the deity of Christ.

As I've mentioned, by the time of the Reformation the ship of the church was absolutely covered with barnacles—saints' days and whatnot. The Reformers scraped virtually all of them off, keeping only what they called the "five evangelical feast days"— Christmas, Good Friday, Easter, Ascension, and Pentecost. All five are related to things that *Jesus* did, and so we are not distracted by the Feast of St. Bartholomew's Finger Bone.

Much of what we identify as "Christmas-y" is no more than a century or two old—our idea of a "traditional" Christmas is basically Victorian. This is not bad, although it *can* be bad if you are not paying attention to your heart and wind up judging your neighbor. I refer to Christmas cards, snow, silver bells, electric lights for your house, and a *Saturday Evening Post* Santa with a Coke.

We expect the government of the Lord Jesus to *grow,* and this means that what we do will look quite different from what was done five hundred or one thousand years ago. We may hope that five hundred years from now, it will be even more mature. In the meantime, we walk by faith in the one who is carrying all of human history on His shoulders—taking us home like an errant lamb.

HOW SHALL WE THEN SHOP?

One of the most common laments we hear at Christmas is that the holiday has gotten way too commercial, that everybody is selling holiday junk, that materialism is rampant, and that consumerism is rampaging loose at the mall. But is this concern legitimate?

To raise this question is not to say that greed and so on are actually good. It is not to say that there are no sins of the marketplace, or that such sins are somehow not present during the Christmas rush. It is simply to acknowledge that "received wisdom" like this is often not thought completely through. Christmas is a celebration of the time when the infinite God took on a material body. Should this not have ramifications for how we think about material things? So part of our duty as Christians has to do with how we purchase things. How so?

JOY TO THE WORLD

In this world, joy is a bedrock sort of thing—and not the froth at the top of a wave. Joy is deep satisfaction in the will of God, and this must be coupled with recognizing the reality that God's will is everywhere and in everything. There is no place where we may go and be allowed to murmur or despair because God's will is somehow "not there." In the carol we sing about joy to the world, we are dealing with the reality of sins and sorrows that grow, of thorns that infest the ground, and nations that need to have the glories of His righteousness *proved*. That proof will be found in our faith.

> Wherein ye greatly rejoice, though now for a season, if need be, ye are in heaviness through manifold temptations: That the trial of your faith, being much more precious than of gold that perisheth, though it be tried with fire, might be found unto praise and honour and glory at the appearing of Jesus Christ: Whom having not seen, ye love; in whom, though now ye see him not, yet believing, ye rejoice with joy unspeakable and full of glory: Receiving the end of your faith, even the salvation of your souls. (1 Pet. 1:6–9)

The apostle Peter is exhorting believers who are facing significant trials. We still live in a world filled with trouble, and so what he says to them will apply to us also. When confronted with the weight of manifold temptations, our response should be that of "greatly" rejoicing (v. 6). When we are tried, our faith is tried

(v. 7). Our faith is tried because God is a goldsmith. When the goldsmith plunges gold into the fire, it is not because he hates the gold, but because he loves the gold enough to want to purify it of its dross (v. 7). When the goldsmith beats the gold, it is not because he has contempt for the gold. He has a crown in mind. This analogy applies more to your faith than to gold (which ultimately perishes), and the goal is to have a faith that praises, honors, and glories at the coming of Jesus Christ (v. 7). You have not seen Him, Peter says, but you love Him (v. 8). You have not seen Him, but you nonetheless believe, and you rejoice with joy unspeakable and full of glory (v. 8). You are striving to obtain the end of your faith (which is constantly being purified by troubles), and that final purpose is the salvation of your souls (v. 9).

Christmas should not be treated by us as the "denial season." One of the reasons why so many families have so many tangles and scenes during the "holidays" is that everybody expects sentimentalism to fix everything magically. But Christmas is not a "trouble-free" season. We want the scrooges and grinches in our lives to be transformed by gentle snowfall, silver bells, beautifully arranged evergreens, hot cider, and carols being sung in the middle distance. But what happens when you gather together with a bunch of other sinners, and all of them have artificially inflated expectations? What could go wrong? When confronted with the message of sentimentalism, we really *do* need somebody who will say, "Bah, humbug."

When referring to joy unspeakable, Peter is not referring to someone living in the back of a cave, having mystic fits. That is not what is meant by "joy unspeakable." It is not "cloud of unknowing," or an orgy of pseudo-enlightenment in the back of your eyeballs. These words are written to believers in the midst of persecution and trial. Pain concentrates the mind. Pain tethers you to *this* world, and the rope is a stout one. But at the same time, the grace of God enables you to look *along* the pain, to look down the entire length of the trial, and to see the purpose and point of it all. For the unbelieving observer off to the side, watching you, there is no explanation that can make sense of it. This is how God works. It is His way. "And the peace of God, which passeth all understanding, shall keep your hearts and minds through Christ Jesus" (Phil. 4:7). The peace of God is an invisible shield, one which others cannot see. This is why it passes their understanding. They see *that* your hearts and minds are protected, but they cannot see *how*.

Note that your hearts and minds are not the shield, and they are not set up to protect the peace of God. The peace of God is no frail thing, needing your help to keep it from being smashed. The peace of God is an impenetrable helmet, and *your* contentment is your head. It protects you, not the other way around. Faith is like refined gold, and faith can do this, even though it may do it imperfectly. Gold is gold, even with dross in it. The first round purifies the faith, so that you can see and understand the process. That faith thus purified is prepared for the next round—even if the fire is more intense, or the difficulties more severe. The point is not to avoid the process. So the message of Christmas is not a delusional message. This is joy to the world. We are not pretending that we live in a world that is not struggling under a curse. The doctor who applies medicine to a wound is not pretending the wound is non-existent. The craftsman who repairs a smashed piece of expensive furniture is not denying the damage. His presence presupposes the damage. The refiner's fire does not exclude the reality of dross—it is excluding the dross in another way. The Incarnation is God's opening salvo in His war on our sins. The presence of sin should no more be astonishing than the presence of Nazis fighting back at Normandy. View the world with the eye of a Christian realist. The turning of seasons makes no one better. The gentle fall of snow removes no sin. The hanging of decorations only makes a living room full of sin sadder. As Jesus once put it, "Ye fools and blind: for whether is greater, the gold, or the temple that sanctifieth the gold? (Mt. 23:17). Which is more important, the hat or the cattle? The foam or the beer? The gift or the altar? The gold paper stamp on the Christmas card or the gold coin of your faith? If our hearts are decorated with the refined gold of a true faith, we may therefore decorate everything else. If they are not, then what's the point? Joy is fundamentally realistic—which is why unbelief thinks of it as insane.

GETTING DRESSED FOR CHRISTMAS

Holidays are frequently times when people get trapped by the expectations game. Because everyone around you assumes that the day is going to be "really good," "special," or "fantastic," and is constantly telling you to have a "merry" one, it is easy to assume that having a merry Christmas is an actual possession of yours, and if not a possession, at least a birthright. Consequently, the tendency is to sketch out in your mind what you would like that possession to be like. But it turns out, metaphorically speaking, that you get socks instead of the shotgun, or cookware instead of pearls, and the expectation lost is a set-up for real disappointment. This is one of the reasons why holidays can be such an emotional roller coaster ride for so many, and Christmas is no exception.

> Put on therefore, as the elect of God, holy and beloved, bowels of mercies, kindness, humbleness of mind, meekness, longsuffering; Forbearing one another, and forgiving one another, if any man have a quarrel against any: even as Christ forgave you, so also do ye. And above all these things put on charity, which is the bond of perfectness. And let the peace of God rule in your hearts, to the which also ye are called in one body; and be ye thankful. Let the word of Christ dwell in you richly in all wisdom; teaching and admonishing one another in psalms and hymns and spiritual songs,

singing with grace in your hearts to the Lord. And whatsoever ye
do in word or deed, do all in the name of the Lord Jesus, giving
thanks to God and the Father by him. (Col. 3:12–17)

The text obviously deals with how we as Christians are to live
all the time, and not just during the holidays. But the holidays are
nothing other than what we normally do, ramped up to the next
level. And so as we prepare our hearts for this celebration, ramp
this up as well. Problems arise when we exert ourselves physically,
emotionally, financially, and so on, and we don't exert ourselves
here. Think of this as getting dressed for the season—here, put this
on. What should you put on? Tender-mercies, kindness, humility
of mind, meekness, patience (v. 12). *That* is holiday garb. When
you are clothed this way, what are you dressed for? Snow pants
are for going out in the snow, right? What is this clothing for?
It is getting dressed for forbearance and forgiveness (v. 13). You
are all dressed up and therefore ready to drop a quarrel, and to
forgive as you were forgiven (v. 13). But that is not enough—you
need to put on another layer. Over everything else, put on charity,
which is the perfect coat, the perfection coat (v. 14). When you
have done that, what are you ready for? You are ready for peace
with others, and that peace is saturated with gratitude (v. 15).
You are also ready for some music, and particularly the music of
grace and gratitude (vv. 15–16). And then, to crown all else, you
are dressed for everything—whatever you do, whether in word
or deed, you can do it in the name of Jesus, giving thanks to the
Father (v. 17).

Given the nature of the case, we must get dressed beforehand.
Many Christians know what they are supposed to be doing, and
so they try to do it. And they feel bad when they fail. But for
some reason they don't prepare themselves beforehand for what
they know is coming. They don't know that how they are dressed
for the task is affecting their performance of the task itself. Now,
let us suppose that for the last seventeen Christmases in a row

you have gotten out of fellowship about something—for gifts you didn't get, for lack of adequate enthusiasm for gifts you gave, for lack of adequate help with the meal, etc. Seventeen years in a row. Now, is it possible to tell which day this will happen the *next* time? Sure, it is this next Friday. The twenty-fifth. It is marked right there on the calendar, leering at you. So started getting dressed for it now. You don't really want to be surprised *again*. When you are clothed as you ought to be—in kindness, humility of mind, and charity—you will be able to take more delight in gifts you give freely, than in the gifts you receive. You delight in both, of course, but what does Jesus teach us? "I have shewed you all things, how that so labouring ye ought to support the weak, and to remember the words of the Lord Jesus, how he said, It is more blessed to give than to receive" (Acts 20:35). There are two basic things to remember here. First, giving is better than receiving. Second, this truth is so obviously clear that many people have had to work out complicated ways of receiving—i.e., receiving credit for being so giving (Mt. 6:2–3). As you give, you need to avoid running a trade deficit, with all categories—emotional, physical, and spiritual—taken into account. Remember that gifts are gifts, and gifts are also symbols. And symbols are also layered.

"For even in Thessalonica ye sent once and again unto my necessity. Not because I desire a gift: but I desire fruit that may abound to your account" (Phil. 4:16–17). Or this: "For what is our hope, or joy, or crown of rejoicing? Are not even ye in the presence of our Lord Jesus Christ at his coming?" (1 Thes. 2:19). What is our crown? Is it not *you*?

In giving a gift, *you* are attached to it. In receiving a gift, the blessing that comes to the giver is *your* chief delight. And the *you* that is attached to the gift that is given is either a gift just like the physical gift, or it is a booby-trapped box full of hidden emotional expenses. Do not be like the woman that C.S. Lewis said lived for others—and you could always tell who the others were by their hunted expression. We give gifts, but the gifts also give us, and that is sometimes not nearly so much fun. You give the gift, certainly, but the gift also gives *you*. And it will always give the "you as you are" and not the "you as you appear in your daydreams." And this is why you must prepare yourself for the giving. You don't want the gift to give you, and have that "you" be a cheap toy that doesn't make it through the afternoon of Christmas day.

This is why you must get dressed for the day.

A THEOLOGY OF CHRISTMAS GIFTS

One of the most obvious features of our Christmas celebrations is the gift-giving. How are we to understand this as Christians? What are the pitfalls? Are all the pitfalls obvious? Because our lives are to be lives of grace, and because *charis* means grace or gift, this is something we have to understand throughout the course of our lives, and not just at Christmas. But it has to be said that the machinery of our consumer racket does throw the question into high relief for us at this time of year.

> And when they were come into the house, they saw the young child with Mary his mother, and fell down, and worshipped him: and when they had opened their treasures, they presented unto him gifts; gold, and frankincense, and myrrh. (Mt 2:11)

Gentile wise men from the East sought out Jesus and they worshiped Him. The established rulers in Israel did not—in fact, Herod played the role here of a treacherous Pharaoh, going on to kill the young boys in the region of Bethlehem.

So the first Christmas gifts were given by the magi to the young child Jesus. This happened sometime within the Lord's first two years of life. Because three kinds of treasures are mentioned—gold, frankincense, and myrrh—it is often inferred that there were three wise men. There may have been, but we don't know. What we do know is that the gifts were very costly.

We know what gold is, but what are frankincense and myrrh? They are both aromatic resins, harvested from different kinds of trees. Frankincense was often burned for its smell, and hence the smoke could signify prayer, ascending to God. Myrrh was used in burials (Jn. 19:39), and Jesus was offered some mixed with wine on the cross, which He refused (Mk. 15:23). It was associated with death. From the context of the magi's visit, and the association with gold, we may infer that these were all high-end gifts. All three of these gifts were very expensive—in these verses, Matthew calls the gifts *treasures*.

The relationship between God and your neighbor is not an either/or relationship—"Either you honor your neighbor, or you honor God." When it becomes that, it is the result of a sinful kind of dualism. In any context where grace is necessary and called for, you can of course sin—through being a grump and begrudging the giving of gifts at all (Jn. 12:5), or by giving to your neighbor *instead* of to God (Rev. 11:10), or by giving to God *instead* of to your neighbor (Mk. 7:11).

The way through, the real alternative, is to give to God by means of giving to your neighbor (Est. 9:22). Your neighbor bears the image of God. How can you give to God, who dwells in the highest heaven? You reach up by reaching down, or by reaching across. No gift given here in the right way goes missing in the final tally (Mt. 10:42). With every form of unrighteous mammon, you have the opportunity to extend grace to your fellow creatures, in the hope that they will receive you into glory (Lk. 16:9). But every gift given here in the wrong spirit is just thrown into the bottomless pit, that ultimate rat hole (Lk. 12:34; Jas. 5:3).

We see our relationship to God mirrored in our relationship to our neighbor. The state of the one reveals the state of the other. "And be ye kind one to another, tenderhearted, forgiving one another, even as God for Christ's sake hath forgiven you" (Eph. 4:32). When the two great commandments are discussed, we are told that the second great commandment is "like unto" the first (Mk. 12:31). The Scriptures are explicit on this point. "No man hath seen God at any time. If we love one another, God dwelleth in us, and his love is perfected in us" (1 Jn 4:12). "If a man say, I love God, and hateth his brother, he is a liar: for he that loveth not his brother whom he hath seen, how can he love God whom he hath not seen?" (1 Jn. 4:20).

This does not mean that we are to charge about aimlessly, buying and giving gifts willy-nilly. The grace of God is not stupid, so don't give pointless gifts just to have done *something*. The grace of God was freely given, so don't let a racket run by unscrupulous merchants extort money from you that you don't have. At the same time, merchants are a form of grace to you. How does God get that daily bread to you (Mt. 6:11)? So don't identify crowds with a racket. Crowds do provide an opportunity for pickpockets, but Jesus loved crowds and He fed them. He gave them *gifts* (Mt. 14:21).

We must understand the relationship between cold water and the unspeakable gift we have received. The best gift we can give one another at Christmas time is the best gift we can be giving to one another all the time—and that is the gift of gospel-saturated grace. Gospel means good news, and as I mentioned earlier how God keeps track of cold water gifts, we should always connect this with gospel. What has God given? Let us give the same way, and in the same spirit. "As cold waters to a thirsty soul, so is good news from a far country" (Prov. 25:25).

The Son of God from Heaven is the gospel from a far country. He is the gospel Himself; He is the good news. And we know that His contagious form of life has taken hold of us when we start gracing each other the same way that He graced us. Notice how the great vertical gift and horizontal gifts *must be understood together.*

> For the administration of this service not only supplieth the want of the saints, but is abundant also by many thanksgivings unto God; Whiles by the experiment of this ministration they glorify God for your professed subjection unto the gospel of Christ, and for *your* liberal distribution unto them, and unto all *men*; And by their prayer for you, which long after you for the exceeding grace of God in you. *Thanks be unto God for his unspeakable gift.* (2 Cor. 9:12–15, emphasis mine)

AND ON A PERSONAL NOTE . . .

Just a few personal notes as postscript about what it means to have a wonderful Christmas. This one year, because Christmas fell on the Lord's Day, we had to spread our normal activities out over a couple days, in order to make room for two worship services within eighteen hours. We usually have a Christmas Eve service, which we did this year, but then we pushed our regular Lord's Day service the next morning back an hour.

We normally have a Christmas brunch in the morning, and a big Christmas dinner late in the afternoon of Christmas Day. When it comes to putting on our feasts, my wife is Incredible Woman, but she is mortal—and to have our formal brunch, presents, getting ready for church, worship, returning home, and a formal dinner for twenty-five people all after church would be enough for me to get a visit from the elders. So we spread it out over two days. Christmas this year was too big for one day. Christmas is a good reminder of why celebrating the Lord's Day weekly with a sabbath dinner is so helpful—it keeps you in shape. I cannot honor my wife highly enough—she is a high-octane celebratory sabbatarian. Although we had a great number of people

over, it was about the same number that we have every week as
we mark the weekly Easter, the Lord's Day. I cannot comprehend
how she does it. She is one of the central reasons so many wonderful things are happening.

So we had our brunch Saturday morning, with all our kids and
grandkids, and some friends for company. We had oven omelets,
sausages, cinnamon pull-apart bread, orange rolls, fruit, coffee
and juice, and a lot of laughter. We prepared for the Christmas
Eve service (a joint service with Trinity Reformed at 5 p.m.), and
then after the service all the family converged on our house again
for opening the family gifts. A few years ago, the grandkids developed a tradition of sneaking up on our house for any Christmas
celebration decked out in funny hats. While they approach the
house they sing, for *some* reason, a song out of *Pirates of Penzance*
("with cat-like tread"). Then one year a goodly number of the
hats were from the Council of Nicea because the Merkle clan
every year puts on a play with the other side of their family, and
this year that play involved St. Nicholas confronting Arius at
that great council. So the hats of the bishops did double duty.
We had a wonderful time exchanging gifts. The Wilson branch
of the kids stayed overnight with us, so we had a blast the next
morning watching kids handling abundance and the kindness of
their parents. We then got ready for church (again a joint service
with Trinity), and worshiped our Father and God, in the name of
Jesus, and in the power of the Holy Spirit—and we gladly served
Him from whom all blessings flow.

As I write this, we are about to sit down at our Christmas feast
with my parents, my brother and his family, all our children and
children's children. God is the God of the covenant, and Jesus
came to earth to keep the promise to Abraham, so that all the
families of the earth would be blessed. Our families gathered here
feel enormously blessed, and yet we are just one drop in the ocean
of blessing that God has prepared for this world.

May God be eternally praised, and merry Christmas.

Lesson Five

DAILY MEDITATIONS FOR ADVENT

The buildup to Christmas should be one of anticipation, learning, and glad expectation. When we long for something, we love to think about it, and when we are thinking about something a lot, this is a good time to learn more about it. Just as Christmas is a time of year when mulled cider is welcome, it is also a time when mulled thinking should happen as well. Thinking about Jesus, talking about Him, and reading about Him at the table throughout Advent, are good ways to fill your house up with the right kind of smell. This lesson contains one reading for each day of Advent (plus a few extra for good measure). Advent begins each year on the fourth Sunday before Christmas.

DAY ONE

St. Alphonse the Lesser

From Advent through Pentecost, we commemorate the life of Christ our Lord, marking His arrival in our midst, His life, His death and resurrection, His ascension into heaven, and His outpouring of the Holy Spirit upon His people. Our observance of these days takes up half the year.

Trinity Sunday is the Sunday after Pentecost, and is the eighth Sunday after Easter. It commences the "ordinary" half of the year, extending from Trinity Sunday to the beginning of the next Advent. But in calling it the ordinary part of the year, we have to realize that if what we have been saying from Advent through Pentecost is true, then *nothing* is really ordinary. We live our lives in the light of the triune God, walking in His ways, building on the foundation of the historical events we have marked and commemorated.

As we do this, we should always recall the reason for what we do, and how it began in the run-up to Christmas. Man will mark his days, and he will evaluate it *somehow*. We should want Christians to think of their summers as part of Trinity season, and not primarily as the time between Memorial Day and Labor Day. Civil holidays are fine, and barbecuing some burgers with the family is just great, but these are not the days we want to use to define our lives. We are *Christians*—that is the most important thing about us, and that should be reflected in how we celebrate and mark our days.

Of course, at the same time, we want to avoid the problem of ecclesiastical clutter, the problem of some saint's day or other getting underfoot every time we turn around. With the Reformers, we mark the life of *Christ* and the gracious authority of the triune God. During the first half of the Christian year, remember the five evangelical feast days—Christmas, Good Friday, Easter, Ascension and Pentecost. Do not look for any commemoration of St. Alphonse the Lesser, patron saint of three-legged cats.

When everything is special, nothing is. God wants us to cultivate a biblical cadence and rhythm to our lives, and not a constant pounding.

∞∞∞

Father and gracious God, we thank You for the arrival of yet another season of Advent. We pray that this season would be marked by the disciplines of joy, and we pray that some of that discipline would shape and form the cadences of our lives. We thank You for this, and we pray in the name of Jesus, and amen.

DAY TWO
Story Organizers

Stories organize our lives, and the stories that won't or can't do that are false stories. The stories that orient us, that place us back where we should have been, the stories that bring redemption, are called true stories. They go by other names if you listen to the tellers of false stories—legends, lies, myths, fairy stories. But true stories have authority to overcome the envious carping of the adversary.

This is especially true of *the* true story. The first man and woman were placed by God in a glorious garden, and given the earth as their inheritance. They were told to stay away from one tree—for the time being—and when the serpent worm entered the garden and lied to them, they gave way to the lust of the eyes, the lust of the flesh, and the pride of life. They, and all of us with them, fell into darkness and confusion apart from the life of God, and were expelled from the garden. Since that time, in the darkness outside that garden, as we have told one another stories, they have all centered on some way or other of getting back into the garden—but it never seems to work.

But the Lord Himself promised a way for us back into the garden. Since the serpent had deceived the woman, and brought condemnation into the world by means of that woman, God in His mercy determined that salvation would come through the woman. The seed of the woman would come to crush the serpent's head, and deliver us all from our self-deceptions. Throughout all the Scriptures, God gave us various indications of what He was going to do—by raising up women to crush the heads of the foe and the avenger.

And when the time was full, when the time was right, the Holy Spirit came to a young Jewish woman who was steeped in the sacred stories, and He told her that she was to be the one. And the Holy Spirit caused her to conceive, such that her son would be truly and completely human, born of a woman, and at the same time He would be the divine Son of God. She received the news of the enormous honor that had been bestowed on her in all humility, and she received the news as the handmaiden of the Lord. She bowed before Him, as we do now.

ooooo

Our Father and God, our gracious Lord, we gather before You now as a grateful people. We have been forgiven all our sins against You, and we have been given the gift of forgiving others their sins against us. We thank You for this, the central gift, the gift of Jesus Himself, the gift of forgiveness. We thank You for this central gift, from which all the other gifts of this season that we may give or receive take their meaning. In Jesus' name we pray, amen.

DAY THREE
Architecture of Time

We are not mindful enough of the architecture of time and history. As Christians, we want to learn to define the course of our lives in terms of the Lordship of Christ. This means defining our year in terms of Christmas, Easter, Pentecost, and more.

The problem with Memorial Day, Labor Day, the Fourth of July, and so on, is *not* that we happen to observe them. There is nothing sinful about a Memorial Day barbecue, but there *is* a problem when such civil holidays supplant and replace our distinctively Christian understanding of time. When *holiday* (holy day) makes people think of secular days, we have a problem.

We are to mark our days in the annual calendar the same way we mark our week as consisting of seven days with one day of rest. We do the same with our historical calendar marked into that glorious division of B.C. and A.D.. The secularists, with their B.C.E. (Before the Common Era) and C.E. (Common Era), are wiser than the children of light. He who defines, wins. They want to win, and so they seek to define. We don't know what we want, and so we tend to just drift along, defining nothing. But it is not the Common Era. There is nothing *common* about it. Jesus Christ made all things new, including how we are to reckon the times. How do we understand our days, our weeks, our months, our years?

The Lord Jesus is the cornerstone, not only of the Church, but also of the history of the Church. He is the cornerstone of time.

ooooo

Our Father and gracious God, we thank You and praise You for ordaining that the history of the world would flow in the ways that it has. We praise You as the architect of all history, and we exult in the building that is being built. And so, Father, in the name of our Lord Jesus, we offer this, our Christmas worship, to

You, and we ask that You would adorn what we offer in the glory of the Holy Spirit. In Jesus' name, amen.

DAY FOUR
Every Calendar Has a Story

One of the most important things we can learn in our celebration of Advent is the foundational truth that calendars are not silent—calendars always tell a story. Now just because a calendar tells a different story from ours does not mean the story is wrong, although it frequently is. But a competing story is always wrong (and idolatrous) when it *replaces* the story, the story of Christ, the story of salvation.

Thus it is not sinful to have a fiscal year beginning in the summer, or an academic year beginning in the fall, or a civil year beginning in January. But it is wrongheaded and very foolish to forget that all these different kinds of years each have a story to tell. And if we listen to these stories long enough, and neglect the story that God has given the Church to tell, we will succumb to idolatry. And then it will seem strange and outlandish to us that the Christian Church marks the beginning of the year in late November, longing for the coming Messiah. "How strange!" The nonbelievers wonder, why would Christians commemorate something like this—God taking on flesh, when "they could be marking really important things, like the start of the fiscal year, or the contribution of labor unions to our society? Why are these Christians bothering us with their trifles?"

It is not surprising that non-believers think this way, but it is shocking when believers are cowed by it. But Jesus *is* the reason for the season. And we are resolved, by the grace of God, not to let competing stories crowd out *this* story. God's people waited for centuries, and then God fulfilled His promises, all His promises. And the world was made new.

ooooo

Father, You have given us the gift of salvation, and we possess nothing that we have not received from You. Like little children at the dollar store buying a present for their father, with money given them by their mother, we are simply returning to You something that You have bestowed upon us in the first place. And yet we do it gladly, knowing that You receive it gladly. We pray with gratitude and delight, and we do it all in the kind name of Jesus, and *amen.*

DAY FIVE
Christmas as War

We continue to prepare ourselves for the celebration of one of the most monumental events of all world history—the time when the Second Person of the Creator God assumed a human body in the womb of a virgin, in order to join us in our sorrow, and to deliver us from it. This element of sorrow prevents us from viewing Christmas through a sentimental and gauzy lens. The killing of the innocent children by Herod is just as much a part of the Christmas story as the shepherds, the wise men, the angels in the sky, or the manger in which the Maker of all things was placed. Jesus came into a sinful world, in which realistic politicians took the measure of the situation, and did what they had to do. The world is a very different place from what it was two thousand years ago, much of it for the better, but we are still taking the lives of inconvenient infants. The work that Jesus came to do, that of throwing down all the idols, is not yet complete.

We do not just prepare for a Christmas full of delightful sentiment, family time, and happy nostalgia—although all these things are acknowledged and embraced by us. We celebrate Christmas, and everything that follows, as an act of war. War? What about peace on earth, good will toward men? Jesus also said that He did not come to bring peace on earth, but rather a sword. How may this be reconciled? Jesus is the Prince of Peace, but the peace He brings is not the peace of dithering diplomats, who like nothing better than talk, talk, talk. Our Lord Jesus does bring peace, but He does so as a conquering king. He brings peace through superior firepower. That firepower is not carnal, but it *is* potent, and the principalities and powers (those that are left) tremble at the might wielded by a faithful Christian church, un-contaminated by idols, worshiping God in the spirit of holiness.

And so we are preparing to say to one another, "Merry Christmas!" And we sing to one another about the inauspicious beginning of Christ's conquest—"Away in a manger, no crib for a bed." But we also see, with the eye of faith, the end of the process—"He comes to make His blessings flow, far as the curse is found." And so in Christmas, we turn to the principalities and powers (those that are left), conduct our celebrations, and all God's people say, "Take *that*."

ooooo

Father and gracious God, we pray to You in the name of the Prince of Peace, the Lord Jesus, who conquered every form of malice and cruelty, hatred and envy, through His death on the cross, and who therefore overthrew war. We confess that we cannot have a war to end all wars, but that You have already done this wonderful thing. We look forward to the time when, through the gospel, we will be able to hang up all our weapons in the great hall, and study war no more. We pray to You in Jesus' name, and *amen*.

DAY SIX
History as Wedding Prep

This is not just a religious festival that we Christians observe. In all that we do in the presence of non-believers, we are making cosmic claims, and we believe them to be true. Put another way, the celebration of Christmas presents a challenge to all the historians and thinkers who want to reckon without Christ, who want to interpret what is going on around them without reference to Him.

But the Bible teaches us the meaning of history. What is it all about? In what context should we seek to understand the Crusades, the Age of Exploration, the Reformation, the Colonial Period, the Industrial Revolution, the War Between the States, the first moon landing? What is the basic context of all this? What are we doing here?

The history of the world cannot be understood apart from the history of the kingdom of God. History must be organized with reference to the Church, the center of the kingdom of God. And what is the kingdom of God like? We have it on reliable authority that the kingdom of God is like a certain king who arranged a wedding for his son (Mt. 22:2). There it is. The history of the world, and of our nation, is *like wedding preparations.*

Sometimes chaotic, sometimes disorganized, but with joy driving it all, the wedding day approaches.

At first we know nothing of it—but then the invitations go out. The Lord Jesus is born of a Virgin, and arrives among us. He proclaims the truth, and a handful start to get ready. He pays the dowry in His own blood, and more begin preparing themselves. The Spirit is poured out, and we realize that the banquet is intended to include *all men.* The preparations will be far more extensive than we first thought, and so we get to it.

Sometimes we get so caught up in the preparations that we forget the wedding, and we lose our place. In such times, it is good to get out the invitation and look at it again. That is what we are doing every Christmas. Unto us a Son is given.

ooooo

Our Father and most gracious God, we are grateful that You have invited us to this wedding. We pray that we would labor faithfully in preparing for the celebration, and that when we arrive at that day, we will be dressed in the kind of wedding garment that only You can give. We are grateful for the perfect and sinless life that Jesus lived, and for how that life began at Christmas, and how it was all lived for us, and on our behalf. We are so grateful, and we pray to You now in the name of Jesus, and amen.

DAY SEVEN
Santa Claus at Nicea

As we continue to celebrate Advent, we need to deal with a competing story. But it would probably be more accurate to say that we have to deal with a godly story that has been encrusted with many layers of foolishness. But let us take away those layers, and ask—who was the original Santa Claus?

St. Nicholas of Myra (a city in modern-day Turkey) was a fourth century bishop. He was renowned for his kindliness to the needy and to children. He inherited a large fortune which he gave away, establishing orphanages, hospitals, and hostels for the mentally infirm. Legends spread concerning his generosity, which included him delivering gifts secretly by night. During his day, the famous Council of Nicea was held and, according to one legend, the orthodox Nicholas slapped Arius in the face for his blasphemy. Following the legend, Nicholas was then defrocked for this breach of decorum, but was later reinstated as the result of a vision. It should be obvious to us as Protestants that some of

the medieval follies concerning veneration of saints were already
at work here.

The man became a bishop, the bishop became a saint (in the
medieval sense), and stories spread concerning his ability to continue on with his generosity, even though he had long been with
the Lord. The stories all had many variations, but generosity was
at the heart of all of them. These different European stories came
to America from many directions, and they all went into our
famous melting pot.

The Scandinavians brought their conception of him as an elf.
The Dutch brought their name for him (*Sinterklaas*). In 1808,
Washington Irving wrote a story of him as a jolly Dutchman. In
1822, a poet named Moore gave us the *Night Before Christmas*,
getting rid of Irving's horses and wagon, and subbing in reindeer
and sleigh. Then in 1863 the famous cartoonist Thomas Nast
gave us the popular conception we see all around us today.

The issue for us is not stockings by the chimney, or other harm-
less customs. But we must learn from this that if we do not tell
our stories *faithfully*, they will gradually change over time until
they become quite unrecognizable. With a story like this—one
that has in the minds of many *supplanted* the story of the Christ
child—we have to remember that St. Nicholas probably would
have slugged somebody over it.

ooooo

Our Father in Heaven, we are so grateful for the story You
have given to us to tell, and retell. We are thankful that the culmination of this story is our salvation, and the salvation of our
children after us. We are grateful for the generosity You displayed
to us in this, and we are grateful also for the imitative generosity that all your faithful servants reproduce in their lives as You
bless them with Your grace. We pray all this in the name of Jesus,
and amen.

DAY EIGHT
Marley's Ghost Notwithstanding

We are *not* here marking the approach of Christmas because the early Christians compromised with paganism. It is not the case that our fathers tried to sanitize some pagan celebration of the winter solstice. As it turns out, the Romans did not celebrate the solstice, and their Saturnalia was on a different day entirely. There was one brief abortive attempt by a pagan emperor to *start* celebrating the solstice (with a feast to the Unconquerable Sun), which was almost certainly a response to the Christian celebration of this day. This day is *ours*, so unbelievers may be cordially invited to keep their hands off it.

At the same time, unbelievers are invited to join us, first as interested observers, then as catechumens, and then as baptized Christians. How do we invite them? By wishing that they would have a *merry Christmas*. No "Seasons' Greetings" for us. Away with "Happy Holidays" and "Holiday trees," And to Dickens' attempt to turn this whole thing into a humanistic, feelgood ghost story, a story which is all about a nebulous spirit of generosity and getting mysteriously un-scrooged, we *do* say, "Bah, humbug!"

Without Christ, we have no Savior. If Jesus did not die, He could not have risen from the dead. If He did not rise from the dead, we are still in our sins, Marley's ghost notwithstanding. If Jesus had not taken on a human body in the stunning event of the Incarnation, He could not have died. If He did not die and rise, we are still in our sins. Without this baby, we are all of us lost, and lost forever.

The war on Christmas is being conducted by those who want no reminders of the potency of this great event. We are here to remind the world that there is indeed joy to the world, the Lord is come. Let earth *receive* her king, and with a little less backchat.

ooooo

Our Father in Heaven, You are the one who forgives sin. You are the one who sent Your Son into this world (by being born into it) in order that He might save His people from their sins. That this was the mission was evident from the very beginning, when the angel revealed that His name was to be Jesus. And so it is in the name of Jesus that we pray, and amen.

DAY NINE
Christmas as Worldview

Worldviews are more complicated than just a simple bundle of propositions. Propositions are of course involved—no one has a worldview who cannot answer questions about what he believes. But in our circles, this tends to be the only aspect of "worldview" that we focus on, teaching our children to answer the specific dogmatic challenges to their faith. This is not to be despised, and never to be neglected, but there is far more to having a worldview than this.

There are three other components that one theologian has wisely noted.[1] They are the elements of narrative, symbol, and practice. *Narrative*—how do we tell the story of what we are doing here? *Symbol*—what forms of shorthand do we use to summarize our beliefs and narrative? And *practice*—how do we live, day to day?

With this in view, we have to recognize how important Christmas is as a worldview issue. In our celebration of Christmas, we are telling the story of world history. Just as the Fourth of July tells the story of independence from Britain, so Christmas tells the story of our successful war for independence from the devil. Christmas, and all the symbols of it (whether trees, carols, or

1. N.T. Wright, *The New Testament and the People of God* (Minneapolis: Fortress, 1992).

Handel's *Messiah*), are markers, monuments built from stone. They are an Ebenezer—thus far the Lord has helped us.

And practice. We order our lives around the life and accomplishments of Jesus. We do this, not so that we might live like pagans in between our holidays, but rather so that these holidays will mark and bound our lives, lives that are lived in the light of the conquering gospel.

And since we believe that the earth will be as full of the knowledge of the Lord as the waters cover the sea, by this celebration we are not only living out our own worldview, we are declaring to unbelievers what the worldview of the entire earth will someday be.

∞∞∞

Father in Heaven, we thank You that in Christ Jesus everything hangs together. We rejoice in the coherence the heavens and earth have under Your sovereignty, and we rejoice equally in the possibility of coherence in our minds concerning the world. We rejoice in the work You began on the first Christmas, and pray that Your Spirit would continue that work in us now. In the name of Jesus we pray, and amen.

DAY TEN
Let Earth Receive Her King

The Lord Jesus was born in 4 B.C., which was the year Herod the Great died. He was the tyrant who had the children slaughtered in the region of Bethlehem because of what he heard from the wise men, and so obviously, Jesus had to have been born before Herod died.

As mentioned earlier, Dionysius the Insignificant was a Scythian who moved to Rome around A.D. 500 and was the first to propose the change of calendar to mark the years since the Lord's birth. Given the resources available to him, he did remarkably well, but nevertheless he was still off by four years. What this means is that (at the time I write this) it has now been 2,016 years since the arrival of the Son of God among us. It has been about 1,983 years since He died on the cross and rose again, ascending afterward into Heaven. From the right hand of the Father, He has continuously ruled the world since that glorious time.

Two thousand years into that reign, that four-year glitch should not trouble us. But if any secularist brings it up as a taunt, we may simply observe that this just means that Jesus has been reigning four years longer than we thought.

ooooo

Father and God, we rejoice in the greatness of our Lord Jesus and in the goodness of His reign. We pray that Your Spirit would continue to work in the world to expand the influence of His realm and reign, and we pray that part of that expansion would dwell in our own hearts and lives. We pray in the name of Jesus, amen.

DAY ELEVEN
The Holiday of Stuff

We are marking our days during Advent, building up to one of the great Christian holidays. This is a potent holiday, one that secularists appear to understand better than we sometimes do. They want to stamp out any vestige of the historic Christian faith in this "winter celebration," and their secularist jihad is not irrational. They know how powerful this story is. This being the case, let us make a point of telling the story in the right way, and very loudly.

In the first place, do not fall for the lie that the spirit of Christmas is an ethereal kind of thing. This is the celebration of the Incarnation, when the eternal Logos of God took on a material body, which He still has. Do not, therefore, join in the general lamentations about "materialism." This is a celebration of God taking on a material body. It is therefore a holiday that should focus on *stuff*.

By stuff, I mean ribbons, decorations, fudge, wreaths, cider, presents, feasting, toasts, shopping with joy, putting up a tree, sending cards, learning a Christmas piece on the piano, and more fudge.

Of course, we all know how to sin with stuff—we were living in a pretty earthy state of sin before Christ came. But He did not come to whisk us out of this world in order that we might go celebrate some kind of Gnostic holiday up in Heaven. We are to honor the Lord Jesus with our stuff. So do not drink too much, do not run up your credit cards, and don't try to buy friends with presents.

But God's answer to sin begins with the Incarnation. We do not escape from sin by denying, or trying to deny, His method for saving us. Our salvation lies in receiving, resting, accepting, and imitating. And how do we imitate? One thing we must do is use *stuff*, and we can only do that by faith.

Father and gracious God, we pray that the thicker we find the world, the more clearly we might be able to see You through it. We pray that you would enable us to see Your splendor in absolutely everything You have given, and that we would also see something of that gracious splendor in the gifts we are picking out for others. Help us to imitate You, we pray, in Jesus' name, amen.

DAY TWELVE
Christmas and Sentimentalism

We must never forget that an essential part of the Christmas story is a stark reminder of the reality of sin. We have already noted that our culture's instinct of marking this holiday by giving gifts, giving lots of stuff, is an instinct that is sound at the base. This is a celebration of Incarnation, of the material embodiment of the greatest Gift ever given. And so of course, we mark and celebrate this with lots of material stuff.

But all our cultural instincts are not quite so helpful. One of the less helpful traditions is the relegation of this entire story into a vat of sentimental goo. Feel-good emotions are the order of the day, and those feel-good emotions are detached from any sense of deliverance from *sin*. We forget that Rachel weeping for her slaughtered children is very much a part of the Christmas story—as much a part of it as the shepherds, and the angels, and the star, and the wise men. This is a story of the infants who were butchered by a tyrannical king, and the one infant who was spared in order to grow up and die for the sins of His people.

This story has death woven through it—the backdrop is death, and sin, and tyranny. We celebrate at this time, *not* because we live in a sentimentalist paradise where there has never been any evil, but only gently falling snow and the sound of sleigh bells in the distance. We celebrate the birth of the one who overthrew the principalities and powers. This is not a holiday that commemorates the essential sweetness and goodness of man. It is a holiday that commemorates the beginning of the story of how it came about that death finally was killed, and how the warrior who did this great thing was spared in His infancy.

This is why the continued celebration of Christmas is a standing threat to the secularists who want to remove every vestige of it from the public square. I dare say they do. They understand it better than we do. *Merry Christmas* really means *tyranny is dead*.

∞∞∞

Gracious Father in Heaven, we rejoice in the deliverance that You have given to us through the Incarnation of Your Son and our Lord, the Lord Jesus. We rejoice further in the fact that the sting of death—guilt under the law—has been removed by Your holy and sufficient grace. We pray in the name of Jesus, and amen.

DAY THIRTEEN
A Decree Went Out From Caesar

As we come to a robust celebration of Christmas, we want to maintain the biblical antithesis. This cannot be done on the basis of genial Unitarian platitudes, eggnog, snowmen, or anything else like these things. "And it came to pass in those days, that there went out a decree from Caesar Augustus, that all the world should be taxed" (Lk. 2:1–7).

So who was this Caesar Augustus? Why does Luke bring *him* into the story? Much more is involved than a simple time indicator. As a young man, *Octavius* (Caesar's birthname) was the adopted son of Julius, and the heir apparent. By the birth of Jesus he had assumed the throne, and was the emperor. In 40 B.C. a blasphemous coin was struck in Gaul which showed the two-headed god Janus, with Julius on one side and Octavius on the other. The inscription said, "The divine Caesar and the Son of God." There was an Egyptian inscription which said that Octavius was a marvelous star, "shining with the brilliance of the great heavenly Saviour." Then, in 17 B.C., a strange star appeared in the heavens, and Augustus commanded a twelve day Advent celebration, a ceremonial embrace of Virgil's statement: "The turning point of the ages has come!" During the reign of Augustus, the cult of an explicit emperor-worship took firm root, especially in Asia Minor. This region was to become the center of persecution of Christians—*and for this precise reason*. Even his taken name indicates the problem. The ruling title *Augustus* was taken by him, which means "worthy of reverence and worship." He was, in short, *homo imperiosus*. Caesar Augustus was simply the last in a long line of ancient men who believed in humanistic empire. But God was sending another kind of emperor, and another kind of empire entirely.

This is what gives force to Luke's juxtaposition. Given what Luke understood about Caesar Augustus, *and* the identity of the Christ, this story from his gospel *has* to be seen as a rivalry of kings. The fact that Christ was born in Bethlehem—thus fulfilling the prophecy of God—as the result of a *command* from Caesar (to tax!) has to be seen as a supreme irony. If the rulers of that age had known what they were doing, they would not have crucified the Lord of glory (1 Cor. 2:8). And of course, the problem was evident even earlier. Had they known what they were doing, Augustus would not have lifted his finger to tax the world. But he only did this because God lifted *His* finger—to save the world.

∞∞∞∞

Father in Heaven, Your goodness to us is eternal, and we thank You for the empire that You have established among men. We thank You for making Jesus the emperor over it, far above every title or name that can be given. We thank You that the empire of Rome is long gone, and every empire like it forever doomed. We thank You in Jesus' name, amen.

DAY FOURTEEN
Glory in the Highest Comes to the Lowest

Jesus was the firstborn son. The expression in Luke indicates that Mary had other children later on (Lk. 2:7), and there is no reason to doubt that those named by Matthew were truly His half-brothers, children of Joseph and Mary (Mt. 13:55).

Where did this firstborn son arrive? There is the famous detail that there was no room in the inn, but the narrative never actually mentions a stable. It simply says there was no room in the inn, and that Christ was laid in a manger (which could even have been outside). Justin Martyr in the second century says that Christ was born in a cave. Constantine the Great had a church built over a cave at Bethlehem, refurbished later by Justinian, which may in fact mark the actual place. Of course, it might not—but it was in that town *somewhere*.

Consider the glory of it all. "Glory in the highest" is sung to dirty and despised men in a field—glory in the highest comes down to the lowest. Glory given to God in the highest is glory given (in another sense) to men in the lowest. In the Incarnation, God condescends to stoop. In the grip of pride, we rarely understand what happened that night. *The highest reached down to the lowest.* The glory goes to God—we do not give glory to God in the highest because we think that something else is "the highest." But when we come to understand the truth, we sing as the angels did. So great joy comes to men—when the order is right, and glory is given to God, *then* great joy can be found among men, *and no other way.*

ooooo

Father over all Heaven, we praise You for a majesty that stoops, for an infinite and incomprehensible humility. We become proud in our conceits and yet You, Creator of all things, were willing to become one of us to redeem us from our sins. We thank and praise You for this, in the name of Christ, amen.

DAY FIFTEEN
Liturgy Shapes

In some Christian traditions, Advent, like Lent, is a penitential season. Now the historical practices of fasting and such related disciplines are not *necessarily* introspective and morbid, and we should acknowledge that they often accompany productive work (ordinations, exorcisms, etc.) instead of producing unhealthy navel-gazing and so on. But we still must be careful.

I grew up in a tradition that gave an invitation every Sunday, inviting us all to become Christians. *The liturgy assumed* that a bunch of us were unconverted, even if nobody else assumed that. And believe me, when you grow up under such a liturgy, you get the message. *You* are quite likely not a Christian, champ. In the same way, penitential seasons, advertised as such, assume that a good-sized chunk of the Christian church needs to afflict their souls over personal sin, and that they need it far more than the Old Testament saints apparently did. They dedicated one day to this task, while we dedicate two to three months.

If the church decided to set aside a month to intensive prayer for world missions, with fasting and dedicated prayer connected to it, and we worked it into the church year, I wouldn't have the same concerns at all. I might well have other questions, but I wouldn't have these.

Do we really want a liturgy that takes a few months out of the year to emphasize that God is impressed when we give things up, just for the sake of giving them up? I am afraid of unintended consequences.

ooooo

Father God, we pray that You would establish us in the true disciplines of the Christian life, and that we would learn to mortify all the stirrings of sin. We pray that we would not allow artificial disciplines to supplant the true disciplines, and that You would do all this in us in such a way as to make us truly glad. We pray in the name of Christ, and amen.

DAY SIXTEEN
Not Recovering Error

Penitential seasons are not necessarily "Catholic." It is quite possible for good, sound Protestants to observe such seasons, provided they redefine everything and do something very different from what gave rise to the historical practice in the first place. But it seems to me this is done with success rarely, and if it *is* successfully done, the question "why?" naturally arises.

The impulse behind penitential-seasons-gone-wrong is the same as the impulse behind purgatory. But the gospel is all about free grace, free all the way, free down to the ground, free *now*. As the old gospel song puts it, "Jesus paid it all." And the untenable nature of certain traditional customs and beliefs is becoming increasingly obvious in significant places. N.T. Wright makes this observation:

> More remarkable still is the view of Cardinal Ratzinger, now Pope Benedict XVI. Building on 1 Corinthians 3, he argued that the Lord himself is the fire of judgment, which transforms us as he conforms us to his glorious, resurrected body. This happens not during a long, drawn-out process but in the moment of final judgment itself. By thus linking purgatory to Jesus Christ himself as the eschatological fire, Ratzinger detached the doctrine of purgatory from the concept of an intermediate state and broke the link that in the Middle Ages gave rise to the idea of indulgences and so provided a soft target for Protestant polemic. Whatever we think of that, it is clear that two of the most central, important and conservative Roman theologians of the last generation [Rahner being the other] offered a quite radical climb-down from Aquinas, Dante, Newman, and all that went in between.[2]

2. N.T. Wright, *Surprised by Hope* (New York: HarperOne, 2008), 167.

This is really interesting, but it should noted in passing that it simply replaces one soft target with another—the magisterium is now possibly down on traditional purgatory, and it seems clear that radical "death by redefinition" is in process for the magisterium as well as purgatory.

So my point is this—for those evangelical Protestants who are engaged in "going back" or "recovering" certain liturgical practices, it is important to make sure that we are not falling into a trap that previous generations of our Christian brothers undeniably fell into. Seasons of penitence, the *way* they have been practiced for centuries (by people who also believed in purgatory for similar reasons), are potentially deadly. Okay, so we found something really cool in the barn. Let's just fumigate it thoroughly before we talk about bringing it into the house.

This does not mean penitential seasons *per se* are equivalent to purgatory, because in a very real sense this life is where the purgation is *supposed* to occur. In other words, there are numerous ways in which repentance, cleansing, sanctification, and so on are *supposed* to be an ongoing reality in our lives. What I am saying is that our liturgical and historical idea of what penitence in the course of a penitential season is supposed to look like was largely shaped by people who also thought that the sufferings of Jesus on the cross needed to be supplemented by us to get the job of our forgiveness done. That is what we need to make sure our seasons of preparation for Christmas and Easter don't in any way perpetuate.

ooooo

Father over all, we rejoice in the free imputation of Christ's righteousness to us, and glory in the fact that You have offered a free and full forgiveness. We know that we cannot supplement that gift in any way, and we know that we cannot impress You by giving things up for no particular good reason. We pray that You would continue to teach us the meaning of this grace, in the name of Jesus, and amen.

DAY SEVENTEEN
His Name Is Wonderful

Isaiah is very concerned with the importance of names. He named his two sons with the future of Israel in mind, and they were both types of Immanuel. And Matthew tells us that the Messiah was named Jesus because He was named Immanuel. And now we come to a glorious pinnacle of naming.

> For unto us a child is born, unto us a son is given: and the government shall be upon his shoulder: and his name shall be called Wonderful, Counsellor, The mighty God, The everlasting Father, The Prince of Peace. Of the increase of his government and peace there shall be no end, upon the throne of David, and upon his kingdom, to order it, and to establish it with judgment and with justice from henceforth even for ever. The zeal of the LORD of hosts will perform this. (Is. 9:6–7)

This passage is still in the same section of Isaiah's prophetic ministry (Is. 7:14), and the New Testament tells us clearly that this passage is also about the Messiah, the Christ of God. This is why Jesus taught in Capernaum (Mt. 4:12–17). And it also shows that the enemies did not know the Scriptures as well as they thought.

> Nicodemus saith unto them, (he that came to Jesus by night, being one of them,) Doth our law judge any man, before it hear him, and know what he doeth? They answered and said unto him, Art thou also of Galilee? Search, and look: for out of Galilee ariseth no prophet. And every man went unto his own house. (Jn. 7:50–53)

But Isaiah had in fact said this just a few verses earlier: "Beyond Jordan, in Galilee of the nations. The people that walked in darkness have seen a great light" (Is. 9:1–2).

Remember the importance of names for Isaiah. He has already named the coming Messiah as one who is *swift to the plunder*. He is also the *remnant that will return*. He is also *God with us*. And because of all this, He is also Jesus, the one *who saves us from our sins*. But Isaiah is not done. He tells us the name of the one who will arise in Galilee of the Gentiles.

∞∞∞

Father over all, we rejoice that You were mindful of the lost condition of all the nations of men, and sent Your Messiah to the Jews so that all men could be saved. We thank You for the great gift given in the Incarnation, and ask You to help us celebrate it right. We ask for this in the name of Jesus Christ, and amen.

DAY EIGHTEEN
Immanuel, Born of a Virgin

As we look forward to celebrating the birth of the Messiah, we want to make sure that we do not falter as King Ahaz did.

> Moreover the LORD spake again unto Ahaz, saying, Ask thee a sign of the LORD thy God; ask it either in the depth, or in the height above. But Ahaz said, I will not ask, neither will I tempt the LORD. And he said, Hear ye now, O house of David; Is it a small thing for you to weary men, but will ye weary my God also? Therefore the Lord himself shall give you a sign; Behold, a virgin shall conceive, and bear a son, and shall call his name Immanuel. Butter and honey shall he eat, that he may know to refuse the evil, and choose the good. For before the child shall know to refuse the evil, and choose the good, the land that thou abhorrest shall be forsaken of both her kings. (Is. 7:10–16)

King Ahaz of Judah was distressed over threats of a confederacy of Syria and Israel (vv. 1–2). Isaiah the prophet was sent to him with a message of encouragement. But before he gave his second oracle, he invited Ahaz to set the terms of it—a prophet of God invited Ahaz to stipulate a sign, and Ahaz refused to do so because he said that this would be "tempting God." Isaiah responded that his refusal, if not tempting God, was certainly *wearying* Him. And so then Isaiah himself gave the sign, which was that a virgin would conceive, have a son, be called Immanuel, and that before this boy grew to years of ethical discernment, the kings that Ahaz was so worried about would both be gone.

Obviously there has to be typology involved in this. Clearly the sign that Isaiah gave to Ahaz was a sign that should be helpful to *him*. If this prophecy is about the birth of the Messiah *only*, this help is difficult to discern. The Messiah was to be born about seven hundred years later. What good did it do for Ahaz to be told that by a particular point, many centuries later, the two threatening kings would be dead? So would Ahaz, and Isaiah, and lots of other people. It is obvious that Isaiah was prophesying that a woman *at that time* would conceive, would name her son Immanuel, and that by the time this boy was weaned, the kings would no longer be a threat.

But this also means that the situation back then was a type of the Christ who was to come. Isaiah prophesied then, the fulfillment happened then, and that fulfillment was itself a typological prophecy. Before Christ was weaned, I wouldn't at all be surprised to find out that Herod was dead.

∞∞∞

God in Heaven, gracious Father, You hold all human history in the palm of Your hand, and it is a small matter for you to arrange for kingdoms to fall before a small child is weaned. We thank You for doing this in such a way as to encourage Your people. Your kindness is eternal, and we thank You in the name of Jesus, amen.

DAY NINETEEN
Broken Body

The body that was broken for you was a body broken on the cross. But the body that was broken on the cross was the same body that was formed in the womb of the virgin. And that body was taken on by the eternal Word in order that it might be broken. The blood that began to circulate in the veins of Jesus before He was even born was the same blood that was to be shed for you many years later.

Christmas is the opening move in God's salvation of His people. As you reflect on the closing moves, the Lord's passion and death, mediate on the fact that they are to be understood all together, as part of the same story.

The obedience of Jesus on the cross can be distinguished from His obedience throughout the rest of His life, but it cannot be separated, just as His body in life and in death can be distinguished (easily), but never separated. If the body that was suckled by Mary was a different one from the one that died on the cross, we are all still in our sins.

ooooo

Father, Your purpose was to save us through none other than Jesus, but it was also Your glorious purpose to save us through all of Jesus. We thank You for the body that Mary cradled, and we thank You that it was a body given to her . . . so that it might also be given to us. We pray in the name of Jesus, and amen.

DAY TWENTY
How God Honors

God does not honor in the same way men honor. He seeks out the lowly. Recall that the first two groups to hear the glorious message of the realized gospel were dirty shepherds at work, and distinguished Gentile astrologers from afar. Let's consider the shepherds. These flocks were probably connected to the sacrifices in Jerusalem. The shepherds were part of a despised class (not even allowed to testify in court cases). This was because they were thought to have sloppy views on the important difference between *mine* and *thine*. But in this, the honorable Jews had become like the Egyptians of Joseph's day, who disdained Jacob and his shepherd household.

At any rate, an angel appeared to the *shepherds*. The angel came, and glory with him, and the shepherds were greatly afraid. The angel declared the gospel, the advent of a Savior for all people. This is a message of *great* joy. And how will you know which baby he is? There will be only one baby in Bethlehem, wrapped in swaddling clothes, and lying in a manger. Then a host of angels appeared and sang the doxology. Glory and *peace* are sung by the heavenly host, the heavenly *army*, and yes, the text doesn't explicitly say they *sang*. But when you look at the words, it is impossible to conceive of the message being reasonably delivered any other way.

At that, the heavenly host receded—the angels resumed their place in the heavens. The Greek verb indicates they remained in sight the entire time they were receding (Lk. 2:15). Think of what the stars look like when a spaceship is going into hyper-drive. And so the shepherds go to find out—the shepherds made haste, and found just what the angel had said (v. 16). They become the first human proclaimers of Christ (v. 17), and then return to their tasks (v. 20). And Mary remembered it all—the source that Luke used for this story is probably none other than Mary herself (v. 19).

ooooo

Father and God, we thank You for sending the angels to announce the glory of our salvation to shepherds. We know that

Jesus came to seek and to save that which was lost, and we thank You that this was evident from the very beginning. We pray to You now in Jesus' name, amen.

DAY TWENTY-ONE
The Strong Man

God sent Christ to bind the strong man. "When a strong man armed keepeth his palace, his goods are in peace: But when a stronger than he shall come upon him, and overcome him, he taketh from him all his armour wherein he trusted, and divideth his spoils. He that is not with me is against me: and he that gathereth not with me scattereth" (Lk. 11:21–23). Luke knows what he's doing here. Matthew records that Herod knew of the threat to his throne. But Augustus knew nothing of it, and Christ came to conquer the world—his throne is David's and His kingdom will never end (Lk. 1:32–33). This is the accusation against Him later (Lk. 23:2). Luke also records the defiance of Peter and John— "Neither is there salvation in any other: for there is none other name under heaven given among men, whereby we must be saved" (Acts 4:12). They are quoting from a coin which ascribed this same saving authority to *Augustus*. The early Christians preached another kind of saving king, contrary to the counterfeit salvation offered by Caesar (Acts 17:7). And we should note in passing that it is no real offense against the magistrate to acknowledge that Christ rules over him (Acts 25:8).

Christmas therefore reminds us of the fundamental antithesis. And in response, we have three basic options—we can affirm the antithesis (by faith alone), we can blur or deny the antithesis, or we can misplace the antithesis. When it comes to the celebration of festivals like Christmas, our role is not to blend in with an unbelieving crowd. What does the holiday mean? It means the kingdom of *God*, not man.

Where do we start? What are we to do? *Begin at the beginning—* do not run before you walk. Remember God's Son, God's word, God's day. *Remember the contrast of kings*—remember the rival saviors. But we have a Savior, which is Christ the Lord (Lk. 2:11). *And here is true potency*—the power we have is in the *name* of our king. There is no other name which brings salvation.

ooooo

Father of all strength, we thank You now for sending us a deliverer, who through His passion on the cross overthrew the strong man, bound him, and took all his treasures. We thank You that we were among those treasures, and that we have now been transferred from the power of Satan to the power of Your kingdom. We thank You in the name of Christ, and amen.

DAY TWENTY-TWO
Below the Poverty Line

We want always to remember and commemorate our holidays like Christians. We must never attempt to recover the "meaning of Christmas" through some generic *Reader's Digest* approach to inspirational stories. The meaning of Christmas is *not* found in a rejection of rank commercialism, but is rather found in the meaning of the whole Bible—sin, promise, redemption, faith and glory. "And it came to pass in those days that a decree went out from Caesar Augustus that all the world should be registered" (Lk. 2:1–20).

We come to a very familiar story—set against an unfamiliar backdrop. Caesar Augustus was an emperor who did not know he was in the hand of God. The prophet had said the Messiah would be born in Bethlehem (Mic. 5:2). And so God turned the wheels of the entire world to bring Joseph and Mary to the right place (v. 1). The first lever pulled was that of Caesar's decree.

The governor Quirinius was governor of Syria twice. The birth of the Lord was associated with his first term. Herod the Great died in 4 B.C., and so we know Christ was born before that time (vv. 2–3).

Joseph and Mary were *poor*. We know this from the circumstances of Christ's birth, and from the fact that they offered up turtledoves after the birth of Jesus (Lk. 2:24). God had promised everlasting rule to the line of David, but just look where that line had come (vv. 4–5). Christ was born in the city of David, but was born in an impoverished household. He was born there because of the decree of the richest man in the world, and so was already ruling from the manger.

ooooo

Great God of Heaven, Your decrees cannot be undone, and by Your decrees You rule all the kings of the earth. We thank You for putting it into the heart of Caesar Augustus to have the whole world taxed, and for the decision to have everyone return to their ancestral homes to register. The inconvenience for Joseph and Mary was great, but we still rejoice that Your Word cannot be broken, and that the Christ was born in Bethlehem. In Jesus' name we pray, amen.

DAY TWENTY-THREE
Five Names

Of course, given the nature of the case, the name of God cannot be understood by us without considering the names of God. We can see this in the name *Elohim*, which carries the plural ending. Using the word *Elohim* to refer to the one God is like saying that we believe in "only one Gods." This reality reflects both the triune nature of God, as well as His infinite majesty. Even with the words of sacred Scripture, the best we can do is point helplessly, and toward great glory.

Isaiah gives the Messiah a five-fold name. His first name is *Wonderful*. We cannot reckon how marvelous God's plan for us in the Incarnation actually is. The second is *Counselor*. God does not just leave us to be staggered by what He has done—He counsels us, He teaches us. The third name is *Mighty God*—remember this is the same God as the *God with us,* Immanuel. The Deity of the Messiah is firmly stated centuries before He comes. The fourth name is *Everlasting Father*. God the Son is not to be confused with God the Father, but at the same time, the Son of God *is* a Father. He is the bridegroom, married to the bride of Christ, the Church. In our corporate capacity, Christ is our husband. As individuals, the Church is our Mother and Christ our Father. He is an Everlasting Father. The last name is *Prince of Peace*. Though His coming has been the occasion of war as the darkness has vainly sought to extinguish His light, in order to keep it from spreading, the long-term result of His coming is necessarily the Peace of God.

Father of Jesus Christ, You have given Him the name that is above every name. In Him, we come to You, and through Him, we are privileged to know You. We thank You for naming Christ, and in that naming, we thank You for naming Yourself. We rejoice in Your salvation kindness, and we rejoice in the name of Jesus, amen.

DAY TWENTY-FOUR
He Will Finish It

The prophet Isaiah teaches us that when the Son arrives, after He is born, He will be given the government and peace. The government will be upon His shoulder, we are told. He will bear up the nations of the world. But this government of His will be no static thing. Of the increase of His government and peace, there will be no end. This accords with what we are told in the New Testament, about how the kingdom of God grows like yeast in a loaf of bread—but it constantly grows. Like a mustard seed, it grows to great size.

> This will be the result of Christ sitting on the throne of David. He will rule over His kingdom, and as a result, judgment and justice will be established forever and ever. This throne of David is at the right hand of God the Father, where Christ will reign until He has put all His enemies under His feet (Ps. 110:1).

This is all of grace; it is not the work of autonomous man. The Lord of hosts, the God of battles, *He* will accomplish this. More than this, His zeal will accomplish this. The salvation of the world is not something that He does half-heartedly. This will be done through His zeal which, given the nature of the case, must be an unflagging zeal. God did not set out to save the world through the government of His Son, only to get tired of the project later on.

What He has begun, He will finish.

ooooo

Father of the Lord Jesus, Father of the First and Last, we thank You that You are the Father who finishes. We rejoice that You have begun a good work in us, and that You have promised to finish it. We thank You that You have begun a good work in the world, and that You have promised to finish that as well. We rejoice to finish our prayer, with that heart, and in that spirit, in Jesus' name, amen.

DAY TWENTY-FIVE
Handmaiden Miracle

So what does Isaiah mean by his prediction that a virgin would give birth? How are we to take this prophecy? We should first consider the words of Matthew.

> Now the birth of Jesus Christ was on this wise: When as his mother Mary was espoused to Joseph, before they came together, she was found with child of the Holy Ghost. Then Joseph her husband, being a just man, and not willing to make her a publick example, was minded to put her away privily. But while he thought on these things, behold, the angel of the Lord appeared unto him in a dream, saying, Joseph, thou son of David, fear not to take unto thee Mary thy wife: for that which is conceived in her is of the Holy Ghost. And she shall bring forth a son, and thou shalt call his name JESUS: for he shall save his people from their sins. Now all this was done, that it might be fulfilled which was spoken of the Lord by the prophet, saying, Behold, a virgin shall be with child, and shall bring forth a son, and they shall call his name Emmanuel, which being interpreted is, God with us. Then Joseph being raised from sleep did as the angel of the Lord had bidden him, and took unto him his wife: And knew her not till she had brought forth her firstborn son: and he called his name JESUS. (Mt. 1:18–25)

What are we to learn from this? First, the prophecy is applied by Matthew, unambiguously, to Mary and Jesus. Whatever the initial fulfillment was centuries before, the primary fulfillment is here. Second, the name Immanuel is equated with Jesus, and we are told the meaning of both names. Immanuel means "God with us," and Jesus means "saving the people from their sins." These two names must be understood together. As Ahaz was delivered from his troublesome kings, so the kings of the earth who trouble us will be no more. Why? God is with us, and we are therefore forgiven. Third, the Greek word for virgin here is *parthenos*, which means virgin. The Hebrew word is *almah,* which is less specific. But in the LXX, a Greek translation of this passage uses the word *parthenos.* The Bible teaches the virgin birth of Christ, and the Greek translation of the Old Testament explicitly taught it *before* the birth of Jesus.

The virgin birth is an important "handmaiden miracle," pointing to the central miracle itself, which is the Incarnation. The thing that should stagger us is the "God with us" part, and not the virgin birth. The virgin birth points to this greater miracle. And because God is with us, thus we are saved. There is no other salvation, no other way, no other forgiveness.

ooooo

Father, You are the one who determined to visit, and to visit us in such a way as to deliver us from our sins. We thank You for that, and we thank You for the lesser wonders, like the virgin birth of our Savior. We thank You for what it teaches us about the greater wonder—the wonder of God for us, and God with us. We rejoice before You in Jesus' name, and amen.

DAY TWENTY-SIX
Balaam the Seer

One of the most familiar elements of the Christmas story is the star of Bethlehem. But at the same time, it remains one of the most unknown features of the story—because unlike the wise men, we don't really look straight at it.

> I shall see him, but not now: I shall behold him, but not nigh: there shall come a Star out of Jacob, and a Sceptre shall rise out of Israel, and shall smite the corners of Moab, and destroy all the children of Sheth. (Num. 24:17)

The prophet Balaam was a covetous and sinful man (Jude 11; 2 Pet. 2:15). But at the same time, even though he was not of the nation of Israel, he was a true prophet. The Spirit of the Lord really did come upon him (e.g., Num. 24:2). Balak, king of Moab, had Balaam summoned in order to put a curse on Israel. In spite of everything, the Spirit of the Lord refused to let Balaam prophesy disaster for Israel—it kept coming out as blessing (Mic. 6:5). Balak was understandably peeved with Balaam (Num. 24:10), but Balaam calmed him down by giving him some very practical and carnal advice . . . for a fee (Rev. 2:14). As a result, the women of Moab enticed the Israelite men into idolatry and fornication, and God dealt with them severely (Num. 25:1–3). Balaam was eventually killed by the Israelites when they invaded the land (Josh. 13:22). Judging from the number of times it is referred to explicitly, both in the Old Testament and the New, this is a very important story.

And in the Christmas story, we most likely have an *implicit* reference to it. At the end of his exchanges with Balak, Balaam gave the words of the text above, and as a prophecy of blessing for Israel, we should be careful to ask what it means. The first fulfillment of these words came with the reign of King David four hundred years later. He was the one who struck Moab (v. 17), not to mention Edom (v. 18). David was the king who was a type of the great king, the Messiah, the Lord Jesus—so Jesus is the antitype, the final and complete fulfillment of this word. A star shall come out of Jacob and a scepter out of Israel, and He will establish His reign. The scepter would stay with Judah until Shiloh came, and He would be the one who would gather all the people to Himself (Gen. 49:10).

∞∞∞

Father, we are in awe of Your sovereignty, a sovereignty that can speak through an ungodly man like Balaam, promising a blessing for Your people for centuries to come. We know that You draw straight with crooked lines, as when You arranged for the treachery of Judas to accomplish our salvation. We thank You for the treachery of Balaam, which was used to announce our salvation so long ago. In the name of Christ we pray, and amen.

DAY TWENTY-SEVEN
Not Very Starlike

Balaam was a prophet, but he was not a prophet of Israel. He was from the east, and was of the heathen nations there. The wise men who came to search for Jesus because of the star were also from the east. It is likely that Balaam's words had been preserved outside of the Hebrew Scriptures—note how the wise men speak of this (Mt. 2:2). They appear to have had much more information than could be gleaned from looking at a star in the sky, even if they were *serious* astrologers. Balaam had prophesied of a king, one with a scepter. The wise men asked about a king. Balaam had specified that this king would be from Jacob, and the wise men asked about a king of the Jews. Herod, the man they asked about it, was originally an Edomite, one of the peoples that this prophecy described as being conquered by the coming king. And, most noticeably, Balaam spoke of a star, and the wise men came in response to a star.

Incidentally, we don't know for certain that there were three wise men—that is simply an inference from the three types of gifts they brought (Mt. 2:11). There could have been six wise men, for all we know—one for each end of each box.

One of the reasons we don't look too closely at what the text says about our star is that it might mess with our modernist cosmology too much. The text says that the star, the same one which they had seen in the east, led them from Jerusalem to Bethlehem, a distance of about six miles, and that the star then stood still

over the house where Mary and Jesus were (Mt. 2:9, 11). Either
the wise men were being "led by" the star in some astrological
sense, meaning that they were doing some incredible math (also
unmentioned in the text, by the way), or a star actually came
down into our atmosphere and did some very unstarlike things.
But why should this be a surprise? A whole host of stars did the
same thing for the shepherds (Lk. 2:13).

ooooo

Father, You gave the command and the whole heavenly host
came into existence. You spoke the word, and they descended
to announce the birth of Your Son to the shepherds, and one of
them descended to guide the wise men to the house where Jesus
was. We thank You for the cosmos You created, and for how
wonderfully You put it together. We thank You for how little we
know about it still. In Jesus' name, amen.

DAY TWENTY-EIGHT
When the True Scepter Is Established

The star over Bethlehem is not what we were expecting. If we
don't accept the astrological math option, then that means the
star came down into our sky, and stood over a particular house—
fifty feet up, say. Does faithfulness to Scripture require us to
accept absurdities? That a flaming ball of gas, many times larger
than our entire earth, came down into Palestine in order to provide first century GPS services? And that it did so without incin-
erating the globe? As I've mentioned earlier, we need to take a
lesson here from our medieval fathers in the faith, brought to us
via Narnia. "In our world," said Eustace, "a star is a huge ball of
flaming gas." "Even in your world, my son, that is not what a star
is but only what it is made of."

If we can leave our bodies behind when we go to Heaven, why cannot a star leave its body behind to come to earth? But any way you take it, the Christian faith flat contradicts the truncated cosmology of moderns. Choose for yourselves this day whom you will serve. And if you choose the wrong way, you are going to have to stop sending Christmas cards.

But remember what the star meant. Balaam is talking about what will happen to all the tinpot monarchies when the real kingdom arrives, when the true scepter is established. In the book of Revelation, Jesus identifies Himself with His ancestor and subject, King David. He is the root and offspring of *David*, and He is the bright and morning *star* (Rev. 22:16). Balaam was talking about what was going to happen in "the latter days" (Num. 24:14), and he is very clear about the rise and fall of nations before the Messiah would come. First, the Amalekites would perish forever (v. 20). After them, the Kenites would go down (Num. 24:22). They would be followed by invaders from Kittim (the Greeks, under Alexander), which is what verse 24 is talking about. But then the Greeks would fade away (v. 24), which is what happened when Rome ascended. And thus, when Rome was on the top of its game, a decree went out from Caesar Augustus, that all the world should be taxed (Lk. 2:1).

ooooo

Father of every scepter, we rejoice in Your intention to establish Jesus Christ as the Lord of lords and the King of kings. We know that His arrival here was announced in great glory, rejoicing over an ever greater humility. We thank and praise You for all of it, in Jesus' name, and amen.

DAY TWENTY-NINE
Killing and Dying

So Caesar gave the command in order to *tax* the whole world (Lk. 2:1). The star gave the command that magi from the east would voluntarily come, bearing *gifts* (Mt. 2:11). Augustus won his throne through a great deal of killing at the battle of Actium. The Lord Jesus won His throne at the battle of Golgotha, where He conquered and crushed the devil by dying, and not by killing. The star in the east, the one the wise men followed, was a star that declared a coming kingdom, a kingdom that would never end. This is the kingdom of the true king, before whom the most magnificent kings in the history of the world were but flickering types and shadows.

Note the contrasts. Taxes are coerced from the populace, for kings are afraid that if they weren't mandatory, then no one would pay them. But the first tribute that came to Jesus was tribute borne by traveling aristocratic foreigners, who were under absolutely no obligation to bring their gifts—other than the internal obligation that God had given them. The difference between these two forms of taxation can also be seen in how these rulers undertake their rule. Augustus insisted that taxes be paid to him. Christ came down to insist that the fundamental payment be made by Him. And because He humbled Himself freely, God saw to it that tribute flowed to Him freely and without coercion.

The star of Bethlehem is therefore the regal emblem of a scepter, a scepter of never-ending glory. That glory is the glory of free grace, which means that we are ruled in liberty. We give in the same way that the wise men did, out of sheer gratitude.

ooooo

Father, we thank You for the gift of being able to give thanks to You. The Lord loved us first, and this is why we love Him in return. We thank You that our tribute is necessary, but given in true liberty and freedom. We are a grateful people, and we thank You in Jesus' name, amen.

DAY THIRTY
Martha at Christmas

In the famous story of Martha and Mary, Mary was sitting at the feet of Christ, listening to Him teach, while Martha was in the kitchen, cumbered with much serving. Jesus said that Mary had the better part, but a lot of us are secretly sympathetic with Martha.

As our Advent preparations come to a close, this is a good thing for us to remember. There has been shopping, cleaning, inviting, cooking, preparing, wrapping, and more. In all of these things, we need to ask God to make Mary and Martha into one woman.

In order to celebrate the right way, a lot must happen, and it doesn't just happen by itself. Work is involved, and the work extends beyond the ordinary levels of work. This means that our understanding of the relationship between grace and works will be thrown into higher relief. If that understanding is sound, then Christmas will highlight it. If our understanding is in any way warped, this means that the holidays will just accentuate that misunderstanding. This is why many families actually dread the holidays.

But Jesus died and rose, and He has sent His Spirit. We have the opportunity to labor in the kitchen and also to sit out in the living room to listen to the Lord's conversation.

ooooo

Father, we rejoice in the arrival of yet another Christmas celebration. We rejoice that we have the opportunity to tell the world that their Savior reigns. We thank You that we are privileged to undertake this celebration with solids, with material stuff. But because it is material, we are often tempted to get distracted with material concerns. Give us an incarnational spirit we pray, in Jesus' name we pray, amen.

CPSIA information can be obtained
at www.ICGtesting.com
Printed in the USA
BVHW031913101022
649092BV00007B/111

9 781591 281276